For Anne,
with best wishes,

Marianne Hardgreaves

28.10.91

THE ALIEN YEARS
The Sequel to *The Naked Years*

Also by Marianne MacKinnon:

The Naked Years (Chatto and Windus, 1987)
The Naked Years (Corgi, 1989)

THE
ALIEN YEARS

The Sequel to *The Naked Years*

Marianne MacKinnon

The Book Guild Ltd
Sussex, England

The characters portrayed in this book are real and the events
described took place, but fictional names have been used in parts to
protect the privacy of those referred to.

The Book Guild Ltd.
25 High Street,
Lewes, Sussex

First published 1991
© Marianne MacKinnon

Set in Sabon
Typesetting by Kudos Graphics,
Slinfold, West Sussex

Printed in Great Britain by
Antony Rowe Ltd.
Chippenham, Wiltshire.

British Library Cataloguing in Publication Data
Mackinnon, Marianne
    The alien years: the sequel to, The Naked Years
    1. England. Social life. History, 1945–1952
    I. Title
    942.085092

ISBN 0 86332 664 1

Contents

List of Illustrations

*For my sons
and in memory of R.*

'Kann uns zum Vaterland die Fremde werden?'
(Goethe, Iphigenie, 1,2)

I

'England, England, here I come!'
As I stepped ashore, my silent outcry of defiance was gaining in
spiritedness the more firmly I felt English soil under my feet.
Behind me lay a tortuous November Channel crossing in a
veteran freighter which only a divine miracle seemed to have
held together at the height of the storm. At the quayside, a cup
of sweet tea, handed to the greenish-looking travellers by
gentle-faced matrons behind urns and mountains of sandwiches, washed the taste of bile off my tongue and spread balm
in my guts.

It was cold and draughty in the Arrivals hall where my companions and I waited to be processed by Immigration officers
and channelled through Customs. As I inched my cardboard
suitcase forward, my thoughts went back across the choppy
grey waters to the homeland I had left behind: a divided
Germany, bowed down by its recent past and the sheer weight
of the tasks ahead, a country using the goodwill of its occupiers
as crutches and, for will-power and morale, drawing on its
survivors' greed for life.

Also, across the miles, I saw 'the naked years' receding. In my
own small universe, I had known loneliness, cold and hunger,
the fear of death, the threat of rape. I had survived. I had grown
stronger. In passing through a commando-type school of life I
had learnt to fight, to pray and to cultivate an inner garden for
my soul – invaluable aids for making the best of any given
situation.

No, I had nothing to declare. My suitcase contained my
earthly possessions – a few clothes, books, photographs, a
diary. I was wearing my only pair of shoes, my stockings were
darned all over, my bra had grown with my breasts and my
war-time coat carried its threadbare patches with dignity. What

I was bringing into the country were my youth and my zest for life. At last, at the age of twenty-three, I was setting out in search of wider geographical and mental horizons. For the regime under which I had grown up had always kept the view across the country's borders solidly blocked, while after the war I had felt more consciously restrained within the narrow-minded enclave of a West German market town whose Bürgers had swept the war under their carpets with the first sound of the peace-bugle, in order to return to the warm and agreeable lap of collective complacency.

Immigration stamped my passport. The alien was to report to the local police within one week. I said I would, and picked up my suitcase which suddenly seemed to contain nothing but air.

On the way to the boat train nothing escaped my keen eyes: a poster advertising a cigarette which promised a superlative smoke, signs in the neutral language of railway stations, the most un-German sight of men walking with their hands in their pockets and women smoking in public, often talking furiously through half-closed lips, cigarettes dangling from a corner of their mouths. Most strikingly, there was no evidence of dejection and depravity, which during the first post-war years I had come to associate with main railway stations in Germany. No presence of human freaks here, no loitering of dealers in lust, nylons and Lucky Strikes. Not even a broken window pane. Instead, at the station-master's window, there were flower-boxes, which in summer might be filled with geraniums. There were printed time-tables which suggested a functioning railway system, with trains arriving and departing at a given time. Not as in Germany, where yellowed and torn *Reichsbahn*[1] notices were still flaking off makeshift boards, or scribbled announcements advised hopeful travellers of the few running trains, the arrival or departure of which had long turned into a waiting game.

First impressions of the former enemy country whose people, history and culture had not long ago been sullied by Nazi propaganda. Now, the real England would reveal itself to me — the country of Shakespeare and Wordsworth, of bustling cities, dignified towns and sleeping villages, of landscapes affectionately evoked by the English servicemen I had known. Fondly,

[1] German railway.

my thoughts embraced the gentle sergeant whose fighting record had not cooled his passion for English poetry; the officer who in his descriptive tour de force had roused Anglophillic sentiments and an obsession with Oxford in me. Having long been day-dreaming of the moment I would set foot in England, and nursing picture-book images of the country on my pillow at night, I felt the momentousness of this first hour on foreign soil churning pleasurably inside me.

I recalled the English lady chairing the Ministry of Labour committee which had interviewed and selected German women between the ages of 19 and 27 for domestic work in English hospitals or for nursing training.

'It won't be easy,' she had said. 'We need girls who will work hard and earn every penny of their free return fare.' And, adding as for the final test, or giving me a last chance to retract a hasty commitment, 'Don't expect to be welcomed with open arms. Some people won't, or can't, forget.'

The suitcase handle in my hand felt moist. Perhaps, I thought, the English war dead, concentration camp horrors and painful memories of German V2 bombing will stand like a brick wall between me and the people I would meet or for whom I would work. I would have to convince them of my goodwill, of my readiness to modify or renew their image of the former enemy. It would be up to me to break down that wall. For, like each of my forty odd companions, was I not a standard bearer for a Germany which, though cut up and reduced in size, was in the process of rebuilding itself on the most fragile of foundations? Perhaps I had been too young, too preoccupied with the business of survival, to learn to love the country of my birth, as one might form an affection for a beautiful tree with which one grows up against the backdrop of the seasons, and as one might cherish first love or the playgrounds of childhood. Now, at twenty-three, I was old enough to be painfully conscious of the legacy Hitler had left my generation which he had once called 'the prized blossoms of the nation'.

At the thought of what suddenly loomed like a gargantuan task, my stomach recalled the turbulent sea passage and my suitcase felt weighted with stones. Just then, only yards away, a male voice confirmed our German presence, expressed contempt, by spitting out the first syllable, 'Germans!'

And now it was the other Germany, the country of Goethe and Beethoven, black pines, sunflowers and the Berliners' defiant slogan, '*Nun erst recht!*'[1] which made me hold my head high and pull back my shoulders – as standard bearers do.

My mind went back to the smiling tea-lady whose 'Welcome to England, my dear!' had been harp music in my ears, auguring well for the future. And, bless her, it was this greeting which now restored my perspective. After all, what did I expect? A path clear of obstacles? Waltzing movements on a parquet floor? And had I not pleaded to go to Oxford, no matter what menial jobs might be involved?

'I'm not afraid of hard work,' I heard myself telling the recruitment team, and adding for good measure that life in post-war Germany was anything but a bed of roses.

'But would you not consider a nursing career with the kind of education you've had?'

I would not, I said. I was stubborn, determined, riveted to my images of Oxford as to my own Mecca. For in Germany's post-war drought I had thirsted for beauty and learning and stable values. For many months, images of the city's colleges and libraries, its meadows and riverside idylls, had courted my imagination, until my shabby refugee room had shrunk to the size of a bird cage. I realized I was in love with Oxford. I was in love with a place on which I had never set eyes.

'Please, God,' I prayed, as I heaved my suitcase onto the train, 'don't let my expectations turn sour, or reality be too harsh.'

I noted with surprise that the seats of the compartment were upholstered, although we were not travelling first class. I still remembered the hard wooden benches, and the long hours spent in pelvic discomfort, as German war-time and post-war trains steamed feebly towards their destinations, desperately overcrowded with refugees or food-seekers, often running out of coal or being shunted on to side tracks, to allow a military train to pass. Full marks then to English train comfort.

The journey to London, although short, brought new discoveries. A pale sun rising over the countryside and dispersing early morning mist afforded clear views of interminable rows of houses pressed uniformly into resentful proximity.

---

1 'That just makes me all the more determined'.

Backyards, filled with sheds, pens or pigeon-lofts, or turned into miniature gardens, vegetable patches or junk depositories, reflected the personalities or the hobbies of their occupants. And now other features struck me as distinctly 'English' and foreign. For how could anyone from a country which set a single chimney stack on a dwelling house, more like an afterthought, fail to notice the multifarious chimney contraptions on English roofs? And how could I, used as I was to the sight of Germans guarding their privacy behind lace curtains, whether in cities or villages, ignore the blatant lack of such net screens in most of the houses the train was passing at slow speed, or such unaccustomed views as dressing-table mirrors standing monumentally in front of each bedroom window?

'My name is Linde. What's yours?'

So began a fleeting friendship, the kind which brings two young people together, as one senses an affinity of spirit in the other or deduces a common social background from speech and attire. Eagerly we searched for similar points of view, explored each other's hopes and prospects for the future. Perhaps on this first morning in England, with the years ahead looming in the mind like a long-sought, yet ill-equipped expedition into uncharted territory, we both realized that strength lay in fellowship, not in the insularity of the loner.

'What a crossing!' said Linde, 'I still feel queazy.'

'So do I,' I said, wondering whether a cynic might read a certain symbolism into our stomachs having rid themselves so violently of their last German meal.

Linde was of middle height and homely looks. She was soberly dressed in a brown coat and matching beret. Her chestnut hair was cut short, leaving a playful fringe to draw attention to her large, doe-like eyes. Like myself, she spoke an accent-free German. Although my junior by two years, she exuded a maturity which I, effervescent in spirit and impulsive in action, was lacking. I was delighted to hear that she had also opted to go to Oxford, yet I refrained from asking what had prompted her to prefer domestic work there to nursing training elsewhere. Neither did she probe into my own motives. Perhaps her reasons, like my own, were too personal, too ambitious or quixotic, to be verbalized.

The London Hostel, where we were to be registered and administratively processed before moving on to our individual places of work or training, occupied a corner in Hyde Park Square. Its Victorian facade still bore evidence of bomb damage, while the grime-encrusted stuccoed ceilings and marble fire-place surrounds of the rooms still retained the faint aura of once gracious living. In 1946, the terraced building had been used as a transit hostel for Baltic refugees; in 1947 for young Austrians recruited for work in mental hospitals and TB sanatoria. Now the first shipment of German Fräuleins was to pass through, to alleviate the alleged shortage of nurses and hospital domestics in the country.

We were allocated a bed, sheets and blankets, clothes and sweet coupons, as well as five shillings, to tide us over till our first salary in three weeks' time. Then we sat down to our first English lunch – fried sausages, baked beans and 'mash', followed by what the cook called 'Spotted Dick', and over which she liberally ladled a viscous yellow substance that had little in common with my mother's pre-war vanilla sauce, but gratified the sweet-starved German palates.

In the afternoon, being allowed three hours for sightseeing, we split up into small groups and aimlessly wandered off, without maps, without instructions as to how to get to places of interest and back. Perhaps through even a greater oversight, no one pointed out to us the various pitfalls of a city, such as London, where ignorance of a left-hand traffic system might have fatal results, and where foreigners without a reasonable command of English could easily get stuck in the maze of streets or at tube junctions. Where, so soon after the war, looking and sounding ostensibly German, might not be without risk.

The confidence of my own group rested on the five shillings in our pockets and on what we hoped would be the angelic protection of innocents abroad. My ability as a fair English-speaker added daring to our enterprise. We talked German amongst ourselves, noisily, exuberantly, feeling safety in numbers. There were cries of delight whenever something conspicuously 'English' or foreign met our eyes – the cries of children used to the insipid, plaintive sights of post-war German cities. Once or twice someone came close to stepping under a car, which taught us the pedestrian's 'Look Left!' rule the fast way.

Here and there, heads turned and hard looks suggested that England was still at war with Germany.

'Bloody Germans!' an elderly man hissed at us, before ostentatiously turning up his coat collar.

'Look, Germans!' a woman said to her companion at a bus stop, and several English matrons in pot-like hats glared at us, some suspiciously, some with overt curiosity or disapproval. Not surprisingly, our smiles faded, our voices dropped a decibel and we herded closer together. And it was not until a man in his late forties, wearing an officer's overcoat, addressed us, as we stood working out our next move, that our mood recovered and our adventurous spirit returned.

'May I help you?' he asked in German, and falteringly explained that the sights of London were too numerous, to cover in a single afternoon and with little daylight left. Then curiosity took over.

'From which part of Germany do you come?'

'The British Zone,' I replied.

The stranger remembered, smiled.

'I was stationed in Holzminden and Ülzen after the war. And I've been in Hamburg, Bremen and Hannover. What are you doing in London, girls?'

My explanation elicited a long-drawn 'Ah and now you want to see London in three hours! I'm afraid . . .' But then a finger directed, a smile reassured the hopeful explorers, before our friendly Englishman, emulating a salute, merged back into the crowd.

As we made our way through Oxford Street and Regent Street to Piccadilly Circus, I noted every unfamiliar sight with the tingling excitement of a first-time explorer: the luscious red blots of double-decker buses, the shiny black of lumpish taxis; policemen, unarmed, looking smart and efficient. Shop-windows, veritable magnets drawing attention to the abundance, elegance or chromatic scale of their displays. Dickensian-type street vendors, roasting chestnuts or selling newspapers, shouting grotesque vowels into the crowd. And, of course, we could not resist the confectionery shops. At the sight of chocolate, fudge and prettily-wrapped sweets we grew weak, which left us with mere coppers in our pockets.

It had started raining and the lights were dancing on the bonnets of motorcars, wet asphalt and pedestrians' faces. Waving good-bye to the statue of Eros, we fought our way to a bus routed to the vicinity of Hyde Park Square. Meekly, we joined the end of an orderly queue, having been manoeuvred to its tail with no uncertain words by those used to waiting drill, which left me amazed at the discipline of Londoners who would not, as was German practice, cluster around a bus or tram stop, before thrusting towards, and through, the coveted entrance with the urgency of refugees trying to board their last means of escape.

'Why does your Government need us Germans to work as domestics and student nurses?' I asked the soberly-suited lady who accompanied Linde and me to Oxford. 'Don't you have enough English women to fill domestic vacancies or undertake nursing training?'

I had long been wondering about our recruitment, reasoning that at the end of the war a large number of English women, who had been working in ammunition factories and on farms, or serving as auxiliaries in military units, would have been free to redress the staff balance in hospitals.

Above the rattle of the train I could hear the lady thinking hard. It was obvious that she had not been briefed on respective government policy, and did not expect young aliens opting for menial work to have inquisitive minds.

'Well,' she said, her official smile fading off her face, 'we now have a brand-new national health system which is expanding rapidly. New hospitals are being built, new speciality units are being opened, and they all have to be staffed. And, of course, there are still thousands of servicemen who will require long-term nursing care – some for the rest of their lives.'

It was the last sentence which, though free of rancour, cut short my probing into national labour schemes. I lowered my eyes and suppressed a sigh, yet I was far from being convinced that the new health service alone had created so many vacancies that the government had been forced to fall back upon German labour.

2

A Worm's View

It was drizzling when we arrived in Oxford. A short taxi ride took us to the Radcliffe Infirmary, through a narrow street crammed with tiny shops, and along a wet, ponderous avenue over which an early dusk stood poised. Expressing satisfaction at having delivered us safely to what she called one of Britain's famous teaching hospitals, our escort led the way through a network of tunnel-like corridors, boosting our morale with well-meaning platitudes. The domestic supervisor, a lady of majestic bust and deportment, welcomed us with a graded smile. She held out a hand, and I stopped myself in time from bending my right knee in German-style deference to age and authority.

'Hello,' she said, sizing us up, and when her examination revealed nothing untoward, 'How old are you?'

We stated our ages.

'Any health troubles?'

We replied in the negative.

'What does your father do?' she asked each in turn.

'My father is a town councillor,' said Linde.

'Mine was the sales director of one of Krupp's steel companies.'

The supervisor's brows shot up.

'And what did you do before you came over?'

Linde explained that she had been taking a typing and shorthand course before the currency reform in the Western Zones cut short her secretarial ambitions. The supervisor looked surprised and I informed her, as the one with greater linguistic fluency, that in June the Reichsmark ceased to be legal tender and each West German, regardless of sex, rank or occupation, had been paid out fifty Deutschmarks.

'To foot the new Germany economy,' I added, wondering whether she would quite appreciate what effect this reform had borne upon each individual.

'I worked as a secretary and interpreter for American and British military government after the war,' I continued. 'Later I ran my own translation office. But like most other small businesses this folded up as a result of the reform. More recently I held various jobs with local British units.'

By now the supervisor's smile had positively wilted.

'Well,' she said, 'I'm sure you'll find things a little different over here. Just put yourselves behind your brooms and brushes, and do what you're told. You're both intelligent, so you ought to learn fast.'

She handed us a duty time-table.

'You'll be working a forty-eight hour week, with either afternoons or evenings off, plus one whole day a week.' And addressing Linde, 'You'll be on duty in the Nurses' Home across the street. That's where your room is, in the basement. I'm afraid you'll have to share it with another girl, an Estonian.'

Now it was my turn. 'You, Miss, will be working on this section of the hospital. Besides keeping the corridor floor and the sisters' dining-room floor clean and shiny, I want you to give a hand in the scullery and with sisters' meals. You'll have a room to yourself in the attic, next to the dormitories.'

Her finger wagged in the air. 'And I warn you: I'm a stickler for punctuality and cleanliness.'

She waited for her words to generate signs of intimidation on our faces. But we continued to look straight at her, unblinking, sure of ourselves, firm in our intentions to prove our worth to this substantial lady.

A smile mellowed her Valkyrian pose.

'Most of your colleagues are from Ireland. They may not have your . . . eh, background, but with a bit of goodwill you should get on well. As for food, you'll have three decent meals a day – including bacon, sausages, eggs, meat – more than the ordinary British civilian can buy.' And seeing our eyebrows going up, 'Oh, yes, British housewives still have to manage on coupons!'

I stared at the floor. I had no idea that certain foodstuffs in Britain were still rationed, and somehow the responsibility for the notched belts of British people seemed, at this moment, to rest solely upon my shoulders.

The supervisor's smile grew positively radiant. 'Work well and eat well, girls,' she said. 'If you have any problems, come and see me. And now, come along and pick up your dresses and aprons.'

My heart sank at the sight of my room. Box-like, its walls painted a canary yellow, with a single hot-water pipe running along one wall close to the skirting-board, it contained a bed, a bedside locker, a rickety wardrobe and a single wooden chair. Over the bed, the previous occupant of the room had left a picture of the Madonna pasted on cardboard. The wardrobe displayed a single clothes hanger, the broken heel of a red shoe and a dog-eared romantic novel. In the bedside drawer hair clips and cake crumbs further pointed to the hasty or careless vacation of the room. There was no window. Instead, high up on the sloping ceiling and out of reach, a square foot of afternoon gloom filtered through a skylight.

As I sat down on the narrow bed, I shivered. Memories of the first half hour at the Children's Home came rushing back: The dormitory. A gleaming linoleum floor. Blinding sunlight. Rows of white iron beds standing against bright green walls like soldiers on parade – a spotless, creaseless uniformity which does not tolerate any dolls or plush animals as comforters. I am sitting on my allotted bed in a plain uniform dress which scratches under the armpits. Feeling naked in the sudden draught of loneliness, I am aching for my mother, for my teddy bear, for the familiar views from which which my parents' divorce have torn me. And I am bleeding, from where my heart is, for the home I have lost, and which had been many things – chocolate pudding and vanilla sauce, kite-flying, chestnut-carving, games of Halma, Rommé and marbles, good-night prayers and kisses, fresh ham rolls and cocoa, birthday candles, Lanterna Magica slides and my mother playing Schubert on the shiny grand piano . . .

I started unpacking. The first ten years of my life might have ended with a bang. But I was grown up now, determined to make the best of things – and more.

I did not see Linde that evening. Neither did I go down to the domestics' dining-room. Somehow I was not ready yet to face my new colleagues, and breakfast-time, with its inevitable confrontation, would come soon enough. I had a quick wash in a room fitted with rows of steel basins and open shower-cubicles, and once I had removed the traces of its previous occupant, I set about making my room habitable. I covered the metal top of the locker with an embroidered handkerchief and put a small vase on it, which I vouched should never stand empty. I stroked the books I had brought with me like canine companions, and supped on the remains of the Hostel's lunch parcel, before I fell into a dreamless sleep.

A sharp knock at the door woke me at 6 a.m. I raced into the wash-room and was back before the mob burst forth from the dormitories. Seemingly with two left hands I buttoned up my striped cotton dress and fixed the straps of my apron. I took care with my hair, banning every flighty lock. With my face free of lipstick, and smelling of no more than soap and Nivea cream, I set out on my new walk of life.

Linde was waiting for me outside the dining-room. She looked pale, anxious and, despite her plain working outfit, blatantly middle-class.

'I'm starving,' I said. 'Come, let's buckle up our courage. We'll have to face them some time.'

Linde made the sign of the cross and followed me into the room in which all but two seats were taken.

'Good morning!'

Our greeting was crisp, confident and free of accent. Instantly, forks came to rest in mid-air, elbows nudged each other, faces grew insolent. Someone giggled. Then a heavy Irish brogue rose from behind a loaded breakfast plate.

'Here they are the Jerries.'

'Heil Hitler!'

'Look, what we've got here!'

'G'morning, ladies.'

'Ever scrubbed a floor before?'

'Or cleaned shit off toilet bowls?'

Voices, mocking, spitting animosity and class envy at us. Laughter echoing coldly from the ceiling. Linde and I hesitated, unsure of our next move. Being the elder, and feeling conscious of my empty stomach, I went to the kitchen hatch for a plate of bacon, eggs, tomatoes and fried bread. Looking neither left nor right, I steered towards one of the empty seats and helped myself to tea and buttered bread. Perhaps, I thought, by pretending not to have understood, or to be upset about the girls' abrasive remarks, and by affecting a smile, I might assure this unfriendly lot, and the vandals of my image of the Irish, that – German or not – I was potentially a likeable person.

Breakfast took its course. Deprived of the satisfaction of seeing their victims visibly ruffled or fading back where they had come from, and associating our neat looks, clean finger nails, and the way we handled our knives and forks, with offensive bourgeois respectability, our tormentors now set upon a different line of assault. In no time the room filled with slippery innuendos and stories of what Tom or Paddy had done to Mary or Maggy after pub closing-time. In their description of sexual manouevres there was many a word I either did not understand or took to have a different meaning. Thus my unfamiliarity with gutter slang made me think of 'crotch' as 'crochet', the hook and looping work, and of 'cock' as a farmyard rooster.

The appearance of the supervisor put an end to the verbal onslaught. Relaxing authority on her brows and lips, she fluted a 'Good morning, girls', before introducing Linde and me to the Irish force. When she got our names wrong, and we corrected her, everybody laughed, looked friendly and companionable.

'Now, girls,' the supervisor said, sinking back into her overseer's role, 'time you were off.' And turning to a stunted, wiry girl whose short dark hair was badly in need of a comb, 'Nancy, will you take Linde along and show her the ropes. Clean sheets today and a good scouring of the baths. And make sure you can see your faces in the lino.'

Nancy, who had provided most of the ammunition for her colleagues' earlier shock tactics, took her time. She drained her cup, dragged herself up and signalled Linde to follow her, but not without first sticking out her tongue at the supervisor behind her back. Giggling, the rest of the Irish team heaved themselves from their chairs and scattered off to wards, sculleries and nursing staff quarters.

The supervisor waved me towards her, an airy smile fiidgeting on her face.

'First thing in the morning, as soon as the sisters have finished breakfast, will you clear the tables and stack all crockery and cutlery into the washer[1]. Then go and clean the dining-room, tables, floor, the lot. Once you're finished in there, give the corridor floor a good scrub and polish. Think of the floor as a mirror, and put your weight right behind the bumper. Clean floors are part of hospital hygiene. D'you understand?'

'Yes, Mrs . . . '

'Ma'm, if you please.'

'Yes, Ma'm.'

'And after elevenses will you help to polish glasses, fill up cruets, sort out cutlery and lay tables for lunch. Tweeny will show you.

I was wondering whether it would be rude to interrupt the flow of instructions and ask what 'elevenses' were, when the lady's podgy forefinger went up.

'Now, when you're on dining-room duty, make sure your hands and apron are clean, and your hair is tidy. Avoid any unnecessary clattering of dishes, and don't speak to the Sisters unless spoken to. Is that clear?'

'Yes, Ma'm,' I replied, my arms hanging limply by my sides.

'There's a good girl. And now let me show you the closet where we keep the cleaning utensils.'

'What are you looking for?' the supervisor asked, seeing me searching around the cubicle.

'A Schrubber,' I said.

'A what?'

'A scrubbing brush fixed to a handle.'

The supervisor gave a short laugh.

'No such luck, Miss Gaertner. In this country we scrub floors on our knees.'

An hour later, armed with a metal bucket, soft soap and a scrubbing brush, I knelt down at one end of the 25-metre corridor ready for my new work experience. I remembered our maid, Erna, scrubbing the kitchen and bathroom floor in our Berlin flat, without having to lower herself to a kneeling position, which no doubt had accounted for her singing, '*Oh, du lieber Augustin* . . . ', while she worked.

---

[1] a huge dish-washing machine

I wetted my brush.

A week later, the skin over my knees had thickened, my nails were chipped and my hands smelled of soap and disinfectant. Even more disagreeable, the armpits of my dress reeked of sweat. I had not broken a single plate, nor dropped a piece of cutlery, and in the gleam of my floor I was seeing a hint of personal achievement. Off-duty, tired, my body aching to the bone, I was unable to summon up enough energy for a sortie into town. Sometimes, Linde and I would chat after work, in a place where we could not be overheard speaking German. However, before long, an overpowering desire to sleep would drive us to our mattresses.

During the first week time moved viscously, the topography of the outside world grew blurred and my sanguine shoots felt pruned back hard. Life, I summarized, was confined within the diameter of the broom closet.

My first day off. A feeling on waking as if every muscle in my body had been kneaded. I tossed and turned, trying to dispel the after-images of a dream in which I had been scrubbing a floor of infinite length to the tick of a metronome set at top speed by the supervisor, while malicious gnomes with Irish voices were trampolining lustily all over its shiny surface, before one little monster upset my bucket.

The first light was dawning through the skylight, when the dormitory noisily disgorged its inmates. I turned over, savouring the luxury of not having to rise and dress in a cold room by the light of a naked bulb. It was the thought of cornflakes – as yet an unknown breakfast treat in Germany – and of crisply fried rashers of bacon topped with an egg sunny side up, that finally drove me out of bed.

In the dining-room, the Irish staff had reached the toast and marmalade stage. Too late I realized that, like Linde, who also had a day off, I ought to have timed myself more wisely, to arrive after my colleagues' departure for work. I sat down, my eyes shifting between my plate and a wall calendar which still braved a spring scene of crocuses and lime-green fields. Around me, among all the munching and slurping, I appeared to be invisible. Perhaps I was. Perhaps the idea of having two 'bloody Germans' in their midst was no longer titillating to my workmates, or they were simply too lazy to spice up a dismal morning.

I was to know better.

'She looks as if she's had a night on the tiles.'

'Or in a pub.'

'Eh, picked up a bloke yet?'

As usual, Nancy was more outspoken.

'Got yourself laid yet, dear? You know . . . '

A gesture which left nothing to the imagination furiously interpreted the gutter expression and, amid giggles and snorts of laughter, drew forth more comments on certain practices in dark alleyways.

The air in the overheated room was heavy with the smell of neglected armpits and coagulated egg; it was sickly with the breath of salaciousness. I stayed silent, unskilled as I was in the art of making mordant repartees, and lacking the necessary linguistic arsenal, to point out, in the King's English and with cool logic in a haughty voice, that where I came from girls did not pick up men, nor did they frequent pubs, and that alleyways, dark as they might be, were certainly no incentives to the most lecherous of couples in wet and blustery weather.

I dropped my knife and fork, and returned to the sanctuary of my room. In the sparse light, and with no view from a window to provide an external perspective, I was unable to raise my morale out of the pit of misery. Conscious of a growing numbness in body and mind, I undressed and went back to bed where, my head pressed into the pillow, my knees drawn up and my arms curled around my shoulders, I cried myself into a dreamless day-time sleep.

By the time I woke, dusk was gathering again, turning the yellow walls into the colour of clay. How long would a letter from Berlin take? I wondered. For separated though I had been from my mother since the age of ten, and often by hundreds of kilometres, which had curtailed such bonding experience as growing up and bringing up, I knew she would have long posted a letter exuding maternal love (something she always found easier to express via the neutrality of paper) and voicing her apprehension that the first breeze abroad might topple me. And did I like the work? Had I made any friends yet? Was I making sure that I was wearing warm underpants in this nasty November weather? . . .

Suddenly, as if to augment the adult's dejection, I craved for my mother's solicitude like a child, and in something akin to self-flagellation I mourned for the home I had lost over thirteen years ago. And as self-induglence bounced off the bare walls, finding no fixation point, I stared at the fragment of sky above me, willing the Almighty to enter the chapel of my room as long as it would take me to say a prayer and for Him to restore my spirits.

Eagerly awaited, my mother's letter arrived three weeks after being posted. In it she painted a vivid picture of West Berlin, the hungry and paralyzed city which a giant airlift was keeping alive.

'It's as bad as in forty-five,' she wrote. 'There's not enough coke to warm even a single room, and the light comes on for less than two hours a day. As the Tiergarten has turned into a wasteland, with every tree and bush hacked down, people have now taken to collecting horse-droppings, and many brave the ruins in search for firewood. Every morning you wake up, wondering what you'll do for food, for rations fluctuate between 800 and 1,000 calories. There are no trains, and no private motorcars on the roads. Come six o'clock in the evening, Berlin grows deadly quiet, only the droning of the heavy planes overhead continues. This is the 150th day of the Russian siege and the Air Lift. How much longer? we ask ourselves. In the meantime, God bless the Americans! Who would have thought that our former enemies would one day become our best friends? You know, Berliners now call their planes "*Rosinenbomber*", as they are bringing in tons of raisins for Christmas . . . '

Something else kept my thoughts tuned to Berlin. Among some old local newspapers I found an article devoted to a charity concert the famous conductor Wilhelm Furtwängler and the Berlin Philharmonic Orchestra had given earlier that year at the town hall, sponsored by Christian Aid. Headed 'Music and

Goodwill', it spoke of the link between the Christian Aid scheme and the visit of Dr Furtwängler and his orchestra, of the international language of music, which knew no bounds of race, party or creed, and of the objectives of a concert which had not only delighted an apprecia-tive audience with an all-Schubert programme, but was clearly geared towards fostering better understanding between nations. The article further revealed that the renowned orchestra was giving a series of concerts in England, without payment, which surely said much for the goodwill of the musicians. It also disclosed that the members of the orchestra had arrived in their only suits, some of which bordered on shabbiness, and that clothing coupons had been made available to allow them to be more fittingly attired.

I remembered the first time my grandmother had taken me to a Furtwängler concert at the Berlin Philharmonic Hall, before it fell victim to incendiary bombs. Smartly dressed, a gloved finger conducting the first bars of the symphony, her eyes alight with musical anticipation, she had prepared me for the sublime experience ahead. 'Beethoven's Fifth,' she said. 'The theme of the First Movement is "A morning in the country". Listen to the awakening of nature . . .' And I remember a war-hardened audience melting away under the strains of the music, and bidding the sirens, the bombers, not to curtail their listening pleasure.

And never to be forgotten: a unique operatic performance in the Berlin Admiralspalast, where the Deutsche Oper had transferred from their bomb-stricken Schinkel building in Unter den Linden. *The Magic Flute* with Elisabeth Schwarzkopf as Queen of the Night. A seat in the third row of the front stalls. Before me, the tall, lean figure of Wilhelm Furtwängler, coaxing every nuance out of the orchestra with his magic wand. A rapt audience. Berliners seeking refuge in art, in the lifting power of music, before being subjected again to the harrassment of the war and the annihilation around them.

Suddenly, the past opened wider, disgorging memories which left me with a sense of gratitude. For now I was free of fear. I was no longer hungry, no longer shivering with cold. I had a roof over my head and, at the end of the month, a pay-packet. I was also mistress over a new range of physical freedom which, though partly pledged to study, would still grant me sweet permutations.

Meanwhile, there were changes afoot in the Radcliffe's domestic quarters. Linde was transferred to a Nurses' Home in Banbury Road, to assist an elderly housekeeper with her daily chores, and I exchanged my attic room for one on the first floor of the Night Nurses' Home across the road. I was delighted. Though facing north and with no room to swing the proverbial cat, it had a fair-sized window which created an illusion of space and freedom. Indeed, if I stood close to it, looking through the spiralling structure of the fire-escape, I could even spot a piece of sky.

The time had also come to haul down my German flag. Not that it had been hanging limply, but chameleon-like I had adapted to new circumstances and an alien surrounding, accepting my job as a valuable experience that would not stunt my growth.

As the weeks went by, my Irish colleagues began to treat me with the indifference of those who find their stock of derisive comments and shock phrases depleted and the unshakeability of their victim ungratifying. And what point was there in hunting down a hornet without a sting?

It was, finally, not so much a saner outlook than an over-riding sense of boredom which on my next day off sent me flying through the hospital gates and out into the streets of Oxford.

A fresh wind was lifting the dense overnight fog, and in Cornmarket and High Street window-shopping promised little more than a chilling pleasure. Undeterred by the whirling of wet leaves and raking gusts of wind, I set about discovering what the city had to offer in the meagre light. I found cobbled alleys, where history seemed to stand still, high stone walls covered with creepers, wrought-iron gates which marshalled the imagination into the grounds beyond. I ventured into college quadrangles and, back in High Street, peeped through the door of a low-ceilinged pub all wooden beams and shining brass. When the sun finally emerged from behind low-hanging clouds, I got my feet wet, tramping through soggy meadows and along puddle-lined paths. I listened to an orchestra of bicycle bells as students raced through the streets and lanes, and to the quacking of ducks on the restless waters of the Thames.

Marvelling at the fine architecture of colleges, churches and libraries, I longed for spring, for the light that would dress up stone and mortar, and breathe gaiety into streets, colours into gardens. And how I longed to be part, somehow, of that studious community en route to one of the pinnacles of learning!

One day I took my first salary into town. I boosted my spirit with chocolate, and calculated how many pay-packets and clothing coupons I would need to buy that button-through flared-skirt dress which I had seen in Webber's for 51s. 11d. But just before I reached Cornmarket, a huge polished brass plate on a splendid Roman-style edifice caught my attention, and the number of undergraduates hurrying up the steps of the Institutio Tayloriana left no doubt that this was one of Oxford's high seats of learning. Looking neither left nor right, I mingled with the young men and women, followed them into a lecture room, grabbed a seat and searched my handbag for pen and paper. I wondered what kind of enlightenment was lying ahead. For all I knew I might have stolen into a Biochemistry or a Political Economy class. Yet I was hardly able to contain my excitement and, pending the arrival of the lecturer, feigned the boredom of students attending a compulsory class which promised no earth-shaking intellectual stimuli.

More than one surprise was in store for me.

'The delicate essence of Rainer Maria Rilke's magical and metaphorical world . . . ' began the lecturer. I rejoiced. Rilke, my favourite German poet whose '*Letters to a Young Poet*' I had studied like a manual on how to cope with loneliness. His love poem, '*Wie soll ich meine Seele halten . . .* '[1], which I knew by heart, had often moved me to tears whenever I felt romantically inclined or imagined myself to be in love. I congratulated myself on my nerve at having penetrated into one of the inner temples of Academia.

The gowned lady, whose rhetoric would have made her recoil in horror from the low talk which ruled in the domestics' dining-room, soon sapped my confidence. For in analysing Rilke's 'inwardness', in giving examples of his metaphysical and

---

1 'How shall I withhold my soul . . .'

orphic language, his idiomatic lyricism and esoteric mode of communication, she spoke to me as in code. And when, ending her lecture she quoted from Rilke's 'Sonnets to Orpheus', *'Das Unendliche bleibt unbeschrieben zwischen Auf- und Niedergang'*[1], my confusion was complete. I had not understood a single word, but for the best part of an hour, when a dropped pencil would have clanked like a steel girder, neither incomprehension nor bewilderment had knitted students' brows.

I lost no time. An hour later I enrolled for the Cambridge University Certificate of Proficiency In English, an advanced language exam for foreign students, geared to matriculation requirements at British universities. I was given a list of books to read and study, having less than six months in which to prepare myself for an oral and multiple-papers exam.

Fleetingly I queried my own wisdom, for I had never studied an English novel with an eye to critical analysis, nor been required to interpret images in poetry. And since I was working shifts, and my monthly salary, after deduction for board and lodging, laundry and superannuation, came to no more than £9 to £10. I did not bother to inquire about classes which prepared or tutored ill-equipped candidates like myself. I realized I was on my own. Yet here was a challenge, the one for which I had been waiting. Hearing intellectual bells ringing, I steered towards the reading-room of the public library where heads bent over books in common spirit, and where even a whisper or the indelicate turning of a page, sounded like an intrusion.

For weeks to come, on my days off or in between shifts, the library was to become my second home. Here I would bury myself in Jane Austen's *Northanger Abbey* and Thomas Hardy's *Under the Greenwood Tree*, into the poetry of Robert Browning, Tennyson and Keats, and – as yet inaccessible to me, linguistically and thematically – into Shakespeare's *A Winter's Tale*. Happy hours. Hours of mental flight, of drinking at the font of knowledge.

*   *   *

---

1 'The infinite remains unwritten before the rising and the going down . . . '

December arrived with a plethora of church services, sung Masses and Carol concerts. More mundane entertainment was on offer at the Carfax Assembly Rooms where the orchestras of Nat Temple, Oscar Rabin and Ted Heath were billed for dancing. The Town Hall staged a concert of Viennese music and a lieder recital. Newspapers blared forth the news that forty million Germans had each received one pound of raisins as a Christmas gift from the United States, to 'prevent distress and disease', while Britain had to fall back on importing 55,000 tons of dried fruit, in order to ensure a Christmas allocation of twelve ounces per head of population. But whatever national resentment the article implied, it was surely offset that day by photographs of Princess Elizabeth and the royal baby.

On Christmas Eve I attended a carol service for Oxford's German-speaking congregation in the chancel of St Mary's Church. Burning candles, the organ playing 'Silent Night, Holy Night' and whiffs of pine from a tall Christmas tree made the German-ness in me rise in a tidal wave. Memories of peace-time Christmas Eves brought back the smell of wax, ginger and cinnamon pretzels; rooms in which flickering golden light and the silvery shine of lametta infused emotions indistinguishable from the palpitations of sentimentality. Memories of war-time Christmases welled up, frugal in their offerings, bleak with uncertainty or sorrow, and with the 'Peace on Earth' message mocked by pages of obituary columns. All that had mattered then was to be alive and near a loved one. Happiness reduced to a simple quotient, to root level. Perhaps, I thought, it was this which had brought people closer to God, to each other, or to the core of their beings, for a few hours, for a day or two, until the bombs started raining down again, fear grew elephantine, death a reality, and the threat of rape the ultimate humiliation. And now, how bright my voice suddenly sounded . . .

✳   ✳   ✳

'Have you been to one of the dances yet?' asked Luise, the fair-haired Estonian refugee who had been at the Radcliffe since 1947. 'It's good fun, and 2s. 6d. will get you in. Why not come along tonight, Marianne? Most of the girls go on their own, just for the dancing.'

'What are the men like?' I asked.

'Students mostly, bank clerks, shop assistants. All in suits and ties. The bands are terrific. I bet if you've been once you'll want to go every Saturday. And who knows, with your looks you can pick up a date any time. Come on, don't be a bore. Oscar Rabin and his band are playing tonight.'

Luise, who reminded me of Hitler's projected image of '*die deutsche Frau*' as wife, mother, home-maker and custodian of the kitchen range, and who professed to be a devout Protestant, allowed me to witness her metamorphosis from a pasty-faced nurses' dining-room maid to a Carfax *belle*. She reduced the circumference of her waist and hips by means of a lace-up corset, slipped into a low neckline dress with a swinging skirt and worked her silk-stockinged feet into a pair of high-heeled shoes. She liberally applied lipstick and rouge, wielded eyebrow pincers and lash-curlers with the skill of an actress, and finally flung her long hair, which she wore pinned into a demure bun at work, over her shoulders, brushing it until it shimmered in the light. Despite a hint of the coquette, she looked magnificent in a Rubenesque way, and I knew the men at the dance would fall over their feet, trying to secure the last dance with her.

'All right,' I said, 'give me time to change.'

My grandmother would have turned in her grave, my mother, equally rooted in her notions of middle-class propriety, pursued me to the door with raised eyebrows and words of caution.

In the huge ballroom the ladies were sitting alongside one wall, facing a row of young men seated on the opposite side. Boldly or furtively, the males surveyed the female roost, picking their partners for the first dance. And the way they hugged the edge of their chairs, poised for the opening strains of the saxophone, they might have been sprinters waiting for the starter's gun to go off.

I enjoyed myself. Not once was I left to go through the nightmare of being a 'wall-flower', and there was surely something infinitely proper, if not of dancing-school etiquette, about the division of the sexes and the supervision of the dance floor by a commissionaire-type master-of-ceremony, something quaint even about the way the young men raced across the parquet floor to the lady of their choice, intimated a bow and asked for the favour of a dance.

Towards the end of the evening, the nice young man with whom I was performing a Rumba, asked me for the last dance.

'My name is Iain,' he said. 'What's yours?'

'Marianne.'

'I'm reading History. Second year. Do you like dancing?' And a few questions and answers later, 'You have an accent. Where do you come from?'

'Germany.'

'Germany? I say, what are you doing in Oxford?'

My partner's interest in the German Fräulein took on a more perceptible form during the last slow waltz, for which the lights were dimmed and couples practised propinquity. Moving literally on the spot, cheek to cheek. I felt his arousal taking physical shape. I remembered Luise's warning that under some unwritten law conveniently devised by British males, a girl was expected to allow her partner of the Last Dance to escort her home, and not to be so prudish as to reject a good-night kiss as the least reward for such trouble.

Iain fetched my coat, took my arm and steered me through the departing crowd like a husband his pregnant wife. The night was mild and calm, but by the time we said good-bye in Woodstock Road he had not stolen a single kiss or worked his way towards a more intimate confrontation, from which I concluded that the Last Dance rule did not necessarily command strict observance.

'May I see you again?' my young man asked. 'I'd love to hear something about Germany, Hitler and the war. Our syllabus doesn't cover recent history yet. Mind you, I can only treat you to tea and toast in my rooms. We could meet in front of the Carfax Belltower and I'd walk you to my college. By the way, did you know that in the middle ages Oxford citizens and students clashed many times at the Tower in bloody battle?'

'I did not. But I have tomorrow afternoon off, and I could meet you there at three, unarmed, that is without sword, pike or dagger.'

Iain's laughter set the note for my first date in England.

* * *

'What was Hitler like?' Ian asked, turning a slice of bread over on a long fork and toasting the other side against the safety-grill of the electric fire.

We were sitting on a hearth rug. On a tray on the floor: a pot of tea, a package of sliced white bread, a bag of sugar, a pint of milk, a jar of jam and a pat of butter. Although I had not expected an undergraduate to invite me to the Cadena Café in Cornmarket, where afternoon tea came with crumpets, scones and dainty cakes on 'silver' stands, served by a waitress in black dress and a lace-fringed apron and cap, I had voiced no objections when asked to 'take tea' in a student's quarters, something Luise called a shrewd variation on the age-old 'Come up and see my etchings' theme. Being a novice in the art of English dating, I reasoned that a cold winter afternoon, and the monastic ambience with which I associated college premises, did not spell seduction or rape over afternoon tea.

Iain's room, reached by climbing a narrow, creaking staircase, held none of the seasonal bleakness outside. Stuffed with books, shelved, piled up or lying open, it emanated the breath, the voices, the studiousness of generations of previous occupants. It spoke to me of privilege, of intellectual elitism. Of a world in which skies were loftier and the air more refined. Of a world closed to me.

Photographs of rowing and hockey teams, an apple core, unwashed glasses and an overflowing paper basket injected a more mundane note. Seated by the fire, munching buttered toast, and warming my hands on a mug of hot Typhoo tea, I felt safe with an under-graduate whose main concern, for the moment, seemed to be the degree of toasting.

'Tell me something about Hitler,' he asked. 'Did you ever see him in person, and what did ordinary Germans think of him and his policies? How much did you people know about concentration camps, and why didn't anybody do something about the persecution of the Jews? Why, for Christ's sake, when the country was falling apart and one assassination attempt had failed, didn't someone place another bomb under Hitler's ass, if you pardon the expression?'

Under such a bombardment of questions, under eyes which, perhaps naively, invited convincing answers, any notions of romance I might have nursed stole out of the room. I hesitated.

How could my answers possibly match the spectrum of questions? After the war, being too busy with my own fight for survival, I had never seriously probed the recent period of history, let alone studied it in depth. As one of my generation, who had been taught to accept state-formulated concepts without questioning, how could I evaluate the attitudes of my countrymen with hindsight, how pass erudite judgements on their alleged lethargy, their blinkered philosophy or the popular foreign concept of collective guilt? All I was qualified for was to defend the ordinary German who, under the keen eyes and ears of the state, and amid an army of willing informers would have risked his freedom and, increasingly, his life for openly querying or criticizing Hitler and his policies. I could only talk, until the moon came out, about bombing raids, firestorms and house-to-house fighting; about hunger and freezing and refugee treks, and about the fear of rape and atrocities by Russian troops. And what a pity Iain did not ask me about the Hitler Youth, the steely songs, the snappy greeting, the boring lectures . . .

So I did my best, answering his questions subjectively, conjecturely, lacking breadth of vision. Yet if I was letting down an eager student who was seeing in me a chance effectively to upgrade his knowledge on German History, Iain did not show it. Perhaps he suddenly realized that when Hitler came into power I had only just mastered the alphabet and was still giving my vote to my teddy bear. That throughout my years of adolescence the Hitler Youth and Party propaganda had streamlined German thought, a process which did not encourage critical dissection. Perhaps he also understood that the ability to analyse, assess and correlate historical facts comes more easily through scholarly study.

There was a knock on the door. Two fellow-students entered, apologized for the intrusion and were about to withdraw again when Iain called them in.

'Come and join us. Here, meet Marianne from Germany.'

Introductions. Smiles. An instant burgeoning of interest in my person, as the representative of a country, in the study of which it was perhaps difficult to trace cause and effect, difficult also to juxtapose Goethe, Kant, Dürer, Luther or Beethoven with the non-culture of Nazism.

'I say, what was it like in Germany under Hitler and in the

war? Were you in the Hitler Youth? And did you know anything about the concentration camps?'

The young man, called Anthony, adjusted his glasses. Mary, all pink and blonde, made a fresh brew of tea and fetched some biscuits.

'How absolutely fascinating to meet you, Marianne,' she said. 'From what part of Germany do you come? Were you ever caught in an air raid? And what about the Russians? We've heard they were positively beastly towards the women.'

Once again I gave a sketchy outline, but then I was able to expand, by going back to the roots of ordinary life under Hitler and during the first post-war years. I felt I had earned my tea.

'How absolutely fascinating,' Mary repeated. 'Here, have another biscuit, Marianne. But now you must simply tell us what you're finding different over here. I'm dying to know. My father always says that we are such strange people, at least in the eyes of foreigners. Germans are pretty much type-cast over here. If you listen to comedians or watch some films you'd think being German was jackboots, clicking heels, sauerkraut, beer, Wagner and lederhosen. Have you noted our idiosyncracies yet?'

This was my cue. They laughed when I recounted my first impressions on the way from Harwich to London, and when I spoke of such unfamiliar sights as housewives doing their shopping with curlers in their hair, or men protecting their lady companions from the danger of traffic and road sprays, by walking at the curbside and switching lanes every time they cross the road.

'People say "Please" and "Thank you" a lot, and "Sorry" seems to be the most popular word in their vocabulary. I did not realize how polite English people are. They even thank each other for saying "Thank you". And how disciplined: everywhere, queues form naturally, without anyone trying to elbow his way forward or sneaking to the head of a queue – and this without armed police standing by! Do you want to hear more?'

'Yes, please,' said Mary, sitting cross-legged on the floor, her body bent towards me in rigid attention.

'Well, let's take your passion for tea. A cup of tea would seem to be a universal cure for the ills of everyday life. I'm well on the way to becoming an addict myself. But then, your coffee doesn't really taste like coffee. I also noticed that few people ever shake hands. In Germany, this is a full-time job. *"Guten Tag"* here, *"Auf Wiedersehen"* there. If you meet someone, it would be rude not to shake hands, and if you wear gloves, you must make sure to take the glove off your right hand first. Over here a handshake seems to be much more meaningful, not just a ritual or a limp gesture.'

'What do you think of our pubs?'

'Well, some look so charmingly quaint, half-timbered, an inn-sign over their doors, perhaps a brass knocker, – marvellously medieval . . . Mind you, I've not set foot in one yet. You see, in Germany ladies don't go into Kneipen, and certainly not on their own.'

Iain saw his chance.

'Ah, but then our pubs are more than mere drinking haunts. They're a way of life, places to socialize, confessionals, information exchanges, spas for our egos. We'd be lost without our dear watering-holes.'

'What else struck you as being different over here?' asked Anthony, lighting another Woodbine.

I stared at his cigarette.

'The number of men and women smoking, even in the cinema and on the streets. And take my colleagues at the hospital. They have a puff with every cup of tea! By the way, I had no idea that sweets, clothes and many food items are still rationed in this country. I thought Britain had won the war?'

'That's what we thought,' said Iain. 'In fact, there's still quite a bit of war-time austerity around.'

I looked at my watch.

'I'm sorry, but it's time I left. Duty calls. I'm afraid our supervisor believes in the German virtue of punctuality. Thank you for the tea, Iain.'

'Thank you for coming, Marianne.'

'My pleasure,' I replied, English text-book style, then through force of habit I shook hands with Mary and Anthony.

Iain saw me to the gate.

'I'd like to see you again, Marianne, but it's getting close to exams. I'll have a lot of swotting to do over the next few weeks.'

His eyes tore themselves away from my lips. His smile died. His shoulders straightened. His hands remained firmly in his

trouser pockets.
'So long, Marianne.'

*   *   *

Waiting for the dining-room to empty, the Sister slowly drained
her cup and folded her napkin. At the sound of distant church
bells stealing through the windows, her stern features softened
and she addressed me with a smile.

'Marianne, tell me, what do you know about Hitler making
life difficult for the German Church?'

I was lost for words, used as I was to the more stereotype
questions on Nazism and my own experiences in the war. I set
down a pile of breakfast plates on which bacon grease was
beginning to solidify. I wiped my hands on a corner of my
apron.

'I can only speak for the Lutheran Church,' I stammered. 'I'm
a Protestant. I believe Party and SS snoopers used to mingle
with Sunday congregations, and pastors had to be very careful
not to speak out against the state, or say anything that might be
interpreted as subversive.'

'What do you know about Pastor Niemöller?'

'The name rings a bell,' I said, 'but I can't quite . . . '

'Well, let me tell you something about the good pastor. He
was a very courageous man. Your leaders wanted to win
control over the churches and unite them in one Christian
movement. Pastor Niemöller, the papers say, was not willing to
make concessions. He even denounced the regime from the
pulpit, and he paid for it by spending seven years in prison and
in a concentration camp. The reason why I ask you is that the
Pastor is coming to Oxford next week. He'll be speaking at the
Town Hall. I thought you might want to go.'

On the night I managed to secure an aisle seat in the crowded
galleried hall where standing-room was at a premium, and the
Bishop, the Lord Mayor of Oxford, Deans and other dignitaries
were honouring the German guest speaker with their presence.
Presiding, the Bishop of Oxford paid tribute to Pastor Niemöller as the leader of the German Protestant church, and as a

man who had devoted his life equally to the service of the gospel and the freedom of the Christian soul. When the visitor rose to speak the audience froze in reverence and expectation, then prolonged applause broke the silence.

'It is more blessed to give than to receive,' be began, and referring to the distress and misery in Europe, 'My duty and privilege tonight is to thank you for what you have already done to alleviate the sufferings of the German people.'

A gentle voice, not used to speaking to such a large audience, a voice that would have triumphed in prayer over mental and physical torture. As suffering becomes tangible in the hall, for some perhaps for the first time, it sends waves of empathy through my guts. Because I have known hunger and cold, fear and misery. Because I have witnessed the inhumanity of war, learnt how cheap, how precious life can be.

At the end of his talk, the pastor bids the audience, the people of Oxford and the whole of Britain, to make as much contact with Germans as possible. He raises a hand in a humble rather than a pastoral gesture.

'May God reward you and bless you for all you're doing.'

I'm swallowing hard. And I don't know whether it is the evocation of the years which I like to forget, the pastor's own wartime suffering or the realization that after four months in England I am still standing on shaky ground, which brings tears to my eyes.

On his way out, measuring his steps against those of the Bishop, Niemöller's face opens up towards the audience, tries to establish contact with as many people as possible.

I hear myself shouting through the applause, '*Ich komm' aus Berlin, Herr Pastor!*'[1] And now it is too late to bite my tongue, for the pastor has spotted me. Smiling, he stops and walks over to me. Behind him, the procession of dignitaries comes to a halt.

'What are you doing in Oxford, *Mädchen?*' he asks in German.

'I work in a hospital, and I study English in my spare time,' I reply, conscious of hundreds of eyes focussing on me, and of my cheeks flushing from such daring and un-English impulsiveness.

'H'm, that can't be easy,' the pastor concedes, taking hold of

---

[1] 'Herr Pastor, I come from Berlin!'

my hands. 'I hope things will go well for you. May God bless you, my child.'

That evening, white lilies lined my path home, and I went to bed as if God's own messengers had spoken to me.

An inhospitable March wind and lusty rain showers stalled my further exploration of the city. One afternoon, taking a break from my studies of prose and poetry, and trying to distance myself for a few hours from corridor floor and scullery duties, I went to see the film '*Quartet*'. Afterwards I treated myself to tea at the Cadena, with my hair freshly shampooed, and dressed as for a date in town.

Around me, wearing timeless suits, or classic-style pullovers graced with strands of pearls, hatted ladies of all ages were sipping tea, nibbling buttered bread or delicately spearing morsels of cake. Conversation was *sotto voce*, and tips were left discreetly under saucers. Except for the eminently more tactful manner of tipping, I could have been in one of Berlin's genteel pre-war Cafés on the Kurfürstendamm, where clocks did not strike and patrons celebrated the coffee–and–cake hour at marble-topped tables and under the light of palatial chandeliers.

On the day clothing coupons ended, I bought the red tartan taffeta dress which I had been coveting for some time, a purchase which left me with the price of a ticket for a Cyril Stapleton Dance at the Town Hall.

I wore my new dress for the occasion. I lacked no partners and I collected compliments as I had once gathered horse-chestnuts as a child. Yet, as had become my custom lately, I sneaked out of the hall before the Last Dance imposed its ritual commitment.

One Sunday morning I attended an Anglican service in St Mary's church, feeling very much a stranger to kneeling pads, choir boys, velvet offertory bags and a liturgy during which my thoughts strayed to mundane matters. It was the vicar who finally claimed my full attention, by handing out bible messages like life-belts, and not stoning the congregation in his interpretation of the Holy Scripture, nor treating those in the pews like primary-school children, as I had known some German churchmen do.

In bed that night I read Rilke's *Das Stundenbuch*[1], and though I could not plumb his 'inwardness', and might often be cast adrift on the choppy waters of a stanza, I found a soothing rhythm in lines which, for me, celebrated a philosophical, spiritual evensong.

Linde invited me over for afternoon tea.

'I have something to tell you,' she said.

Her face was radiant. As she poured the tea she announced, more in the way of an aside, 'I'm getting married at Easter.'

'You're what?' I exclaimed.

Linde was not to be ruffled. 'His name is Roger. He is a lecturer in Italian at New College. Will you come to my wedding at St Aloysius? We're both Catholics.'

'Where did you meet?' I asked.

Linde was evasive, or so I thought.

'I've known Roger for some time. Here, have another doughnut. More tea?'

I was wondering whether the quiet, self-possessed Linde, who might not turn a man's head in the street but would no doubt make an exemplary wife, housewife, mother and companion-in-marriage, had perhaps met Roger while he had been serving in Germany where, although fraternization had been in full swing for some time, British government policy still made affairs of the heart between servicemen and German Fräuleins stop short at the church or the registry office. Forcing myself into the private affairs of a person, friend or not, was, however, not one of my vices, and after five months in England I was familiar with the adage that 'curiosity killed the cat'. Experience had also taught me long ago that there are certain things one doesn't like to share, because sharing might detract from their quality. So I probed no further.

'I'm very happy for you,' I said, conscious of a pang of envy, as the perennial seeker after love and a home.

Over a third cup of tea we discussed bridal matters, such as the colour, fabric and style of Linde's wedding dress. And as dusk fell, we ventured into the pre-nuptial field where questions and answers often flow more easily between friends than between mother and daughter.

1 The Book of Hours

'When will you be stopping work?' I asked, when Linde had switched on the light and drawn the curtains.

'At the end of the month. Everything has been arranged. We'll use the Easter break for our honeymoon.'

'I bet your wedding will set some tongues wagging.'

Linde shrugged her shoulders. No more. She was twelve days and one mile away from the altar, the movement suggested, also twelve days from a new social standing.

'And where are you going to live?'

'In Bishop King's Palace, down at St Aldate's. A lovely old building, dates back to 1530. It was once the residence of the first Anglican Bishop of Oxford. Later, the Catholic Church acquired it. We've been given a flat there. It's absolutely mediaeval, wood panelling, creaking stairs, sloping floors and window sills . . . I love it.'

There was a glint in her eyes, and I knew she had already broken with bucket, scrubbing brush, Vim, soft soap and duster.

During Easter week Linde got married. She wore a calf-length taffeta dress of the palest cream, a choice which exhibited German thrift and practical considerations inherited from the years of clothing coupons, and which formed a happy compromise with her brown hair and eyes. The long ceremony included Mass, during which I had ample time to reflect on Linde's good fortune and the radical changes her marriage to an Englishman and a member of an Oxford College would bring. I marvelled at the ease with which she performed her part in the wedding rites, and as she walked down the aisle on Roger's arm, her smile embracing her love for the man beside her and the church's sacred commitment, I knew that she would integrate into English society and an elitist community not only without bruising, but by contributing in her quiet, mature way to what the press called 'a policy of rapprochement between Britain and Germany', and Pastor Niemöller had termed 'a greater understanding between the Christians of two countries.'

After the ceremony, prompted by an acute Easter week staff shortage, I went straight back to work, the wedding and, not inappropriately, a Shakespearian Sonnet I had been studying on my mind. The corridor floor beckoned. But rather than profaning thoughts about incense, vows and wedding bells, it encouraged ruminations about love and marriage.

My scrubbing brush was moving over the floor to the leisurely rhythm of 'Let me not to the marriage of True Love/ Admit impediments. Love is not love/Which alters when it alteration finds/Or bends with the remover to remove . . . ', when a voice startled me from behind.

'More elbow grease, Miss Gaertner, if you please!'

'Elbow grease?' I asked innocently, looking up at the tower of disapproval, yet remembering all too clearly how the recruitment lady in Germany had tried to inject realism into my dream of going to Oxford, by not mincing her words: 'It'll be hard work. You'll need a lot of elbow grease . . . power behind your scrubbing brush.'

'Faster, faster,' the supervisor explained. 'It'll be lunchtime soon.'

'Sorry,' I said, and for the length of a stanza wielded my brush *molte vivace* to the rhymes of Tennyson's *The Lady of Shalott*:

> 'On either . . . side . . . the river . . . lie . . .
> Long fields . . . of barley . . . and . . . of rye, . . .
> That clothe . . . the wold . . . and meet . . . the sky; . . .
> And thro' . . . the field . . . the road . . . runs by . . .
> To many . . . -towered . . . Came . . . lot;'

The months of May heaped superlatives upon Oxford. Spring green and a profusion of wild flowers rejuvenated its river banks, lawns burst into lush carpets. In parks and gardens, trees vied with each other's white and pinks for arboreal beauty crowns and activated painters' brushes and poets' pens. Exams were in the air. Students cycled faster, gowns flapping, taking corners with a verve bordering on recklessness. Frequently, word escaped into the non-academic world of locked-out night revellers or spring-inflamed Romeos sneaking back over college walls, in the process often risking more than a torn trouser leg. One fine spring night an inebriated soul climbed St Giles's statue for a bet, finding himself glued to the top with a sudden attack of vertigo.

Roger and Linde had settled down in Bishop King's Palace, and

I often dropped in for a cup of tea and a chat.

Roger, a very personable man in his early thirties, had fought in Italy during the war. He had never been to Germany. Attractive in an Italian way, but without the easy charm of the Southerner, he was of medium build and a friendly, gentle disposition. I took to him immediately.

'I wonder why your government recruited so many foreign women for hospital work and as trainee nurses?' I asked one afternoon when we were seated around an open fire in the living-room, where slants and creaks galore, lattice windows, heavy wood panelling and carved oak furniture readily transported the visitor into earlier centuries.

'And Germans for all that,' I added. I was adamant. For on this afternoon I stood firmly on mid-twentieth century ground.

Roger, lighting a pipe, gave me leeway to expand.

'I realize your new health system may open up new vacancies, but think of the army of young Englishwomen whom the end of the war must have freed for the labour market. It doesn't make sense. Couldn't hospitals have easily absorbed them?'

'A good question, Marianne,' said Roger. 'The recruitment of foreign labour puzzled quite a few people in the beginning. But look at it like this . . . '

As if he were chairing a tutorial, Roger examined the subject under discussion. He spoke of the twelve thousand and more people reported to be on the hospital waiting list in the area of the Oxford Regional Hospital Board alone. Of the necessity to staff new units, with modern techniques requiring a higher staffing level.

'What you don't read in the papers is that nowadays young women don't like to go into domestic service any more, and unless they are strongly motivated few will opt for a nursing career.'

'Why is that?'

'Much smaller pay packets, an all-female environment in hospitals, a new attitude to menial work, the inevitable narrowing of personal freedom . . . ' And he explained that many women had worked in factories and in the armament industry during the war, where they had performed a man's job, often holding responsible positions and earning good wages. One argument made particular good sense to me: the reluctance of former members of the Armed Forces to fill domestic and nursing vacancies. For in serving their country they had gained new experiences and new horizons, they had enjoyed a good pay, fringe benefits and, perhaps quite significantly, male comradeship and companionship.

'There would have been less bitching, less envy than in an all-female institution,' said Roger. 'Also greater opportunities to find a husband. Besides, I've read that forty out of every hundred student nurses fail to complete their courses. So all things considered, I'm not surprised that hospitals are crying out for domestics and nurses.'

'They must be desperately short to recruit Germans,' I blurted out.

Roger grinned.

'Ho, what's this? A chip on your shoulder?'

'A large one, I'm afraid, which brings me to my Irish workmates.'

'Ah, that's a different kettle of fish altogether. You see, the government has to take in a certain quota of Irish labour. From what Linde told me about your dear colleagues, some of the nastier types must have landed at the Radcliffe. Don't forget, Marianne, that most of them come from large and poor families, and from areas where there are no jobs to go round. Most of the girls would be uneducated or ineducable, fit only for the lower end of the labour market.'

Suddenly I looked at my own scene more objectively and from a wider angle, and I knew that in future tolerance would take the edge off my workmates' verbal assaults.

But I had not yet exhausted my zest for information.

'And how are people treating you?' I asked Linde. 'Do you find much antagonism at the university – I mean, among Roger's colleagues?'

Linde shook her head and looked to her husband for an erudite assessment of her situation as a former alien. I accepted another piece of cake and sat as attentively as I had in the Taylorian lecture theatre.

'There's been quite a change of atmosphere and attitude at British universities since the war,' explained Roger. 'They've become much more open, a mixed society, short on prejudices and, at least at Oxford, short on anti-German sentiments. All colleagues of mine have taken instantly to Linde. But then, how can anyone not like her?' he added quietly, and the way the couple looked at each other made me feel sore with envy.

'It's true,' said Linde, returning her attention to her teatime guest, 'everybody I've met so far has been very friendly. Perhaps a few questions here and there. You can hardly blame people. And can you believe it, I've quite taken to the English way of life.'

A letter from Eric, the gentle sergeant and lover of poetry, who had been the first Englishman to occupy a romantic niche in my life after the war, traced me to the Radcliffe. He was going to break his journey on his way up north, and could we meet?

Since he had only one hour between trains, Eric was not fussy about the venue for our Wiedersehen. A grubby little café near the station had to do: a listless waitress, bare table tops, tea and cakes that did not invite patrons to return. An atmosphere in which memories of Gandersheim, the small West German market town, did not come rolling back, to fasten on to the present, no flashes of the Clausberg, Wordsworth poetry, daffodils or a balmy June night under the stars . . .

Out of uniform Eric looked smaller and his rugged soldier's complexion sallowed. Even his eyes, which had once startled me with their cornflower-blue, mirrored post-war fatigue. Civilian life, so even his voice, his bent shoulders, the slow gestures intimated, showed no respect for medals, nor for a man's poetic flight. It had flagged his spirit. It had grounded him.

'No, Marianne, I did not go back to university. I'm training to be a nurse.'

'A nurse?'

'Yes, we have male nurses in Britain.'

'Are you still reading poetry?'

'Not much time for it nowadays. But what about yourself?'

As the minutes ticked by, I felt the gulf between us widening, and I knew that even at the Cadena, with its muted clatter of cups and spoons, and more palatable offerings, no bridge would have spanned it.

Eric had changed. So had I. And the longer we sat, groping for words, the louder screamed my own apologies: Don't you see, there have been other men. I am no longer the girl you once knew. I am walking taller. I am thinking taller. I have outgrown my Gandersheim self.

I saw Eric back to the station.

'I shall never forget you, Marianne,' he said.

Respectful of the brief happy chapter in our lives, which had refused resurrection, I waved goobye until we lost sight of each other. Then, to dispel the sadness in my system, I briskly walked through the town down to the river, where the meadows and the fast-flowing water formed a suitable background against which to ponder over the fickleness of time and human nature.

*   *   *

My mother wrote that the Blockade had been lifted. And now that the Soviet siege had come to an end, there was every indication that the future supply of goods to the city by rail, road and waterways would be guaranteed. Money was still short, and so was food, while shopkeepers, not quite trusting the new Deutschmark, were rumoured to be holding back vital goods. But then no one knew what else the Russians might have up their sleeves. The kitchen sink had been blocked again, and did I remember the last time it had needed a plumber?

'You couldn't get one for love nor money. Now, there's no shortage of plumbers or men who will undertake any job for Deutschmarks.'

She was growing tomatoes on the balcony, my mother wrote, and she had had to take in her dresses several centimetres around the waist and hip because she had lost so much weight . . .

How far away Berlin suddenly was, how distant even my mother's domestic and personal concerns. For a moment this sense of remoteness pained me, but then I realized how unashamedly a regularly-fed stomach had corrupted me, how readily I had taken to English customs and mannerisms, to Anglican sermons and the golden light of Oxford's spires; how delightedly to the sweet scents of local academe. I also realized how every book, every poem I was studying thrust me deeper into English literary thought and into the English way of thinking. How, finally, without a flicker of regret, this steady conversion, and my insiduous integration into English society, was basically alienating me from my homeland.

*   *   *

My days at the Radcliffe came to an end when I was sent to work at the Headington Manor Hospital.

My room was under the roof, but its fair-sized window faced the greenness and tranquility of a park. I pushed the table under the window and with books and notes transformed it into a desk and a perfect place for study. Exams were less than three weeks away, and I knew I would have to devote every free hour to preparing myself as a candidate with a fair chance.

Once again, as on many occasions during the war, fate intervened in disguise. On my first morning on duty, while making my way down to breakfast, I slipped on the stairs, breaking a bone in my left hand, which henceforth enabled me to apply myself to my studies full-time, albeit with my hand and forearm in plaster and in a sling. And since my mind was no longer required to concentrate on 'greased elbow' tasks, laundry counts and the deft handling of dishes, it jumped at this chance. It literally rejoiced. And the deeper it delved into English eighteenth and nineteenth century literature, the harder it tried to cope with mock epic, couplet and canto, the more audibly it argued with Pope that though a little learning might well be a dangerous thing for some, it might evoke a thirst for more knowledge in others.

Long, lonely days. In front of me, print, behind the retina images galore. Outside, the park inviting tired eyes to swim in its sea of greens. Lonely evenings, bemoaning with Tennyson 'the days that are no more', the poem which in its melancholic mood somehow fuelled my own sentiments and made me go to sleep with my arms cradling my pillow.

The written exams were held on two days, to be followed by an oral. Eagle-eyed supervisors, papers, instructions, a hall tense with the janglings of candidates' nerves.

'Answer the following questions . . . 'Show by reference . . . ' 'Explain the devices of imagery in . . . ' 'Show whether you agree with . . . ' 'Write a critical appreciation of . . . ' 'Explain in your own words . . .' 'Give a summary of . . . '

I listened to an embarrassed silence inside me. What I would not have given at this moment for a third year student's ease critically to analyse, collate and summarize, to spot the obvious and disregard the irrelevant! Dictation passages. A translation from English into German, during which I chewed my pen over the meaning of 'inauspicious' and 'happy augury', before leaving blanks. I found no essay subject to my liking, knowing little about 'Hurricanes', even less about 'Collectors and their treasures', and nothing at all about 'Amateur gardening' and 'The 1948 Olympics' in which Germany had not taken part, and the news of which had been side-swept by the dire impact of the currency reform on the lives of West Germans. And how, with most of it in ruins, could I describe 'The wealth of my country'? I had also never travelled down a 'big river', which would have enabled me to give 'a voyager's account'. Finally, following a tentative assessment of 'The child is father of the man', in which my powers of analysis regressed to primary school level, I wrote 'An imaginary conversation' between the Bishop of Oxford and Pastor Niemöller, backed up by recent facts, figures and sentiments.

In another paper, being unsure of 'Britain's main contribution to world civilization', and in no way qualified to deliberate on 'English traditions', I chose the easy way out, by describing what I had done 'On first coming to England'. Happily, I felt almost on home ground when commenting on Tennyson's 'Tears, idle tears . . . ' as an expression of the poet's frame of mind, as I did for an appreciation of 'Galsworthy's realism in his writing', having read many of his books in German. When the written exams were over, I treated myself to a bar of chocolate and went down to the river where college teams were busy training for Eights' Week, and ducks kept carefully to the banks. Watching fast-gliding bows ripping up the water and paddles striking it in unison, I emptied my mind of all things weighty, until Christ Church tower stood aflame in the sunset and the water had settled again.

My oral examiner was Professor Boyd, a kind-looking man who

put me at ease by first asking general questions about my family and my job. I read out various passages aloud and was asked to comment on their contents. As time passed, my tongue loosened and I engaged in coffee-table conversation.

'Do you know that you have an American accent?' asked the professor.

'I'm not aware of it,' I replied, nonplussed, for had I not tried for months to emulate Oxford English or what they called the King's English?

'Well now, how you would like to come to tea next Sunday, Miss Gaertner? My wife and I would make you most welcome. Four o'clock, if this is convenient.'

'Thank you, professor,' I said. 'I'd love to come.'

I arrived at St Margaret's Road on the stroke of four, a bunch of pink carnations in my hand. Although the weather had taken a most unseasonal turn, I waited around for a few minutes, conscious of German etiquette which decreed that arriving too early for an invitation, or even dead on time, was bad manners and likely to catch the hostess in last minute preparations or with her hair still flying.

The Professor and his wife received me with smiles and a courtesy which could not have been more generous towards a friend or a college Fellow. Their living-room saluted the visitor with an open fire, the softness of cushions, family photographs, books, newspapers and the cosy presence of pink knitting.

I felt immediately at home.

Lightning flashes of memory: My grandmother's salon. A grand piano, gilt-framed paintings, Persian rugs, brocade, lace, long-stemmed roses in crystal vases – all of which required the youngster to have clean shoes and hands, move cautiously and sit erect on silk-upholstered chairs. My parents' comfortable living-room, complete with flowers, gramophone and Gigli records, but also heavy with a wooden silence between father and mother, or discordant with the shrill overtones of marital quarrels . . .

Tea, cucumber sandwiches, buttered scones, a strawberry gateau.

'An English afternoon tea,' Mrs Boyd explained. 'Please help yourself as if you were at home.'

'There are so many things I would like to ask you,' said the Professor. 'About Hitler, the war and your own experiences. You are the first German I've met since thirty-nine.'

'And yours is the first English home to which I've been invited,' I confessed, and Mrs Boyd's maternal smile encouraged me to reach out for another scone.

The professor leaned forward.

'It's the account of an 'ordinary German' which is so interesting. What you don't read in the papers or hear on radio.'

When I left, the couple saw me to the door.

'Thank you for coming, Marianne. It was fascinating to hear your side of things. We feel privileged . . . you must come again.'

I went through the parting ritual of an English tea-time guest. It occurred to me that I had not been asked a single question about concentration camps or gas chambers. Perhaps the omission of that subject had been intentional. In observing the unwritten rules of hospitality my hosts might not have wanted to embarrass me, particularly since my youth, in the eyes of the world, had already pronounced me 'not guilty' on every count.

On a sudden impulse I shook their hands, German-style.

*   *   *

My plaster was taken off and I was certified 'fit for work'. However, before I had time to don my apron, I was transferred as a cleaner to the Nurses' Home of the Churchill Hospital. I said goodbye to names and faces which I had not known long enough or would care to remember, and to a view from my window which had become part of my inner landscape.

At the Churchill I worked on my own, loosely supervised by a Home Sister who would practise her German on me by commenting on the day's weather and on English weather in particular – a topic which I found filled many a conversational void. She also gave me full marks for the gleam of bathroom taps and the corridor's lino floor, and regularly complimented me on my 'fine cup of morning tea'. I did not divulge that prior to coming to the Churchill I had never brewed a pot of tea, apart from war-time and post-war herbal infusions, and that no more than a recent magazine article on the art and the five cardinal rules of English tea-making was responsible for such excellence.

During the day, 'Music while you work' and tunes from 'Workers Playtime', escaping through nurses' bedroom doors or blasting away in their lounge, sweetened my labours or pepped up my spirits. Off-duty, I enjoyed a freedom which did not ask for status and rewarded me in direct proportion to my expectations: A visit to the cinema – two feature films, preceded by Pathe News, a documentary, a cartoon, perhaps a Hammond Organ overture – good value for 1s. 9d. or 2s. 6d. Bus rides into the countryside, walks by the river or through The Meadows. Dancing at the 'Carfax'. Dates. Riverside pubs. A heated group discussion in a student's room at Ruskin College on Marxist theories, pragmatism and the philosophy of a restructured society, during which I figured as a mere listener, soaking up socio-political arguments, whilst admiring the young polemics' motility of thought and geometrics of reasoning. Worcester College gardens on a warm June night – the venue for a performance of *The Tempest*, set against lawned carpets, ancient trees and the reflection of stage-lighting on a small lake spangled with water-lilies. Feeling part of a body of young Oxford undergraduates, of a grass-seated audience seemingly as familiar with Shakespearian lines as if they had been put into their cradles. Shakespeare as outdoor theatre. Language still foreign to the newcomer's ear, yet in its nobility, dramatic power and romantic intonation as gripping and intoxicating as a Beethoven symphony. Or a summer afternoon in a punt. Gliding down the Cherwell under the overhanging branches of elm trees and past the lush lawns of Magdalen College gardens, noiselessly, except for the soft patting sound of the pole and the humming of insects – a romantic dream born in the cold hours of an all too realistic German post-war existence, and flawlessly translated into reality.

Impressions of which memories were made.

＊　　＊　　＊

A letter from Scotland, re-directed several times and finally chasing me across the Channel to my present whereabouts, rekindled a poignant episode of the past.

I had not forgotten the young Scottish Captain who in the end-of-war chaos of a small West German town, had flaunted non-fraternization rules to follow the urgings of his heart. A poet and French speaker, he had even expressed his feelings for me in lyrical form: a poem, written in French, unequivocally titled 'Bien-Aimée'. Yet I had never allowed our romance to develop beyond platonic bounds. Perhaps because I still felt attached to the memory of the young German Hauptmann who had perished in the wintry hell of Stalingrad. Perhaps, raw as the war had left me, I had still been alienated from the concept of a former enemy turning lover. Besides, hungry as I was, with the house I lived in ransacked by former forced labourers and the threat of a secret Russian takeover of the town hanging over my immediate future like a Damocles Sword, how could anything but the lyricism of a relationship transcend the brutality of those first post-war months?

'Please, come and visit us in Glasgow, Marianne,' Alastair wrote. 'I'd love to see you again, and my mother says you'd be most welcome. She's never met a German before. I'm on vacation now, so I could show you around. Do you remember, I once said I would have to update your knowledge of Scotland, which had stopped short at sheep, castles, tartans, Mary Queen of Scots and the Loch Ness Monster? Well, here's my chance.'

I looked forward to my six-day holiday, to being pampered a little, smiled upon and given all the attention reserved for a house guest. Above all, I looked forward to meeting my former boss and hopeful paramour again.

Inevitably, as the train steamed north, my thoughts wheeled back to June 1945, to Tangermünde, the mediaeval town on the river Elbe, which despite hours of heavy street-fighting had escaped the full brunt of war. Following weeks of US occupation, the town had come under the wings of a Highland Light Infantry batallion, with a moustached Captain of smart bearing and what I took to be archetypal English manners, in charge of administration. And I thought of my own exposed position as his interpreter, secretary and English-German liaising instrument, and how the two of us had worked together for the benefit of the town.

Alastair met me at Glasgow Central.

'Hello, Marianne.'

I quickly adjusted my mental image. Before me stood a civilian who had parted with his moustache, which made him look less dashing, and whose shoulders no longer felt the need to square themselves under the weight of a pipped uniform. His smile, however, formed an instant bridge across the years.

'How good to see you again, Marianne. Here, let me take your suitcase.'

During the two-penny tram-ride, which took us to his mother's flat in Hillhead, we filled in the gaps in our lives. While mine had taken a sharp turn in forty-eight, and was now bubbling on without any firm sense of direction, Alastair was now at Glasgow University, reading History and Political Economy.

'Going back to university wasn't all that easy to begin with,' he said. 'I had seen active service in North Africa, Sicily and North-West Europe, followed by a stint in Palestine with my Regiment. My outlook, my way of thinking had changed. Miles seemed to separate me from my fellow-students, most of whom had come straight from school. Some had never been farther afield than Largs or Inverness.'

Alastair's widowed mother, sister of the Lord Provost of Glasgow, received me with a smile that suggested she would reserve judgement on the young lady whom her son had brought to her house, and who – for all she knew and may God forbid – might become her daughter-in-law. The hand that touched mine was cool, but then Scottish hospitality took over.

The days passed quickly. I had little difficulty, fitting into a Scottish middle-class home, and I tried to ingratiate myself with the lady of the house, by making liberal use of 'please' and 'thank you', the national custom which had become second nature to me. To an observer, the alien stood as a fine example of adaptation, having assimilated, copied or bowed to 'English' etiquette and the demands of good manners. But only I knew how willingly I had done so.

To score additional points with Alastair's mother, I laid the table and helped with the dishes. On Sunday morning I accompanied mother and son to a Presbyterian service, at which I sang the hymns as lustily as I had once been taught to render the Nazi anthem. At home, I never exchanged an intimate smile with

Alastair in his mother's presence, nor by gesture or intimation gave rise to any misinterpretation of my feelings. Not that I had to pretend. For, somehow, the chemistry between my former Captain and myself, which had once brightened my lean, lustreless post-war existence, no longer worked. Yet of one thing I was sure: in lieu of love I was able to offer friendship, generously, uninhibitedly – the means by which we might share the libido-freed treasures of our minds. What about Goethe and Frau von Stein? I argued. Had their platonic friendship not borne them a rich mental harvest?

How naive I was. Yet, also how intuitively right.

Gradually, Mrs Warren loosened her emotional corset and now flashed the odd smile at me, which eased the atmosphere at table and in the sitting-room. She even parted with her mother's recipe for apple crumble. When alone, Alastair and I were intent on making up for lost time. We played tennis in Hyndland and listened to *Les Sylphides* on records. We read out and discussed poetry, and on Saturday night went dancing with the 'fast' set at the Piccadilly Club in Sauchiehall Street, where a crowded dance-floor allowed no more than rhythmic on-the-spot movements. We went to see Noel Coward's *Bitter Sweet*, and walked in Kelvingrove Park, talking about life in general and Tangermünde days in particular. 'Do you remember . . . ?' How easy it was to turn the clock back, how difficult to re-set it to the present.

I was invited home for tea by Professor Smith, Head of the German Department at Glasgow University and a friend of the Warren family. The professor, keen on meeting his first German after the war, made me feel like a royal visitor. He poured tea and offered biscuits. Was I sitting comfortably? He fetched a leather-bound volume of Goethe's *Faust* and was delighted when I read out some of his favourite passages in German, my voice suitably tuned in to the drama. However, when the good professor started speaking to me in colloquial German, my eyebrows rose. He repeated the sentence.

'I'm sorry, professor,' I said, hating myself for what I was doing to this sweet, mild-mannered man of learning. 'I don't quite understand . . . '

How easily, how unwittingly one could inflict embarrassment when least intended, I thought, and lowered my eyes.

The professor, bless him, suffered his oral Waterloo with dignity and bonhomie. He explained that over the years rust did not only weaken metal, but that the lack of practising a language abroad, or with native speakers, was bound to affect a linguist's pronunciation. This said, he repeated the sentence in classical German, and smiled when I acknowledged the finely structured syntax. Then he went over to the piano and played Schumann.

'Thank you for visiting me,' he said, on seeing me out. Perhaps you'll come again. Any friend of Goethe's *Faust*, and anyone who can sit as still as you when I'm playing the piano will always be welcome.'

A car ride to the Trossachs in perfect August weather. Here, at last, I fell in love: with lochs and hills and glens, with sights bathed in warm autumn light, with lush greens set off by heather and gorse colours, and with vistas changing at every bend. The clean, bracing air went to my head like champagne, the stillness of places, as yet unspoilt by mass tourism, filled me with an inner peace which made light of the future.

One evening Mrs Warren's voice rose speculatively from the depth of her armchair.

'Did you find the people in Oxford friendly, Marianne?'

Aha! I thought. What she means is: Is there still a lot of ill-feeling towards Germans.

'It depends,' I replied. 'Some folk treat me as if Germany had never been at war with Britain, others see in me the personification of Hitler and the Third Reich. For them, I am the scapegoat for rationing, for V2 bombings, for the loss of a loved one, for the skeletons of Jews staring at them from the papers or the screen. Then again, you meet people who go out of their way to make you feel at home in their country, or who see in you an innocent victim of a political system. And take the students and academics at Oxford . . . '

Alastair stepped in.

'I think there are distinct divisions. The middle and working classes, for all I know, have generally remained solidly anti-German, especially those who lived through two wars. On the other hand, there's a definite pro-German atmosphere at universities, most conspicuously among those who have a sense of history. And similar sentiments exist among ex-servicemen who have fought against Germans, or who were stationed in Germany immediately after the war, particularly if they had contact with German people.'

I grinned.

Alastair's voice rose a merry decibel.

'Of course, here I speak from experience.'

Mrs Warren stole a glance at me.

'Incidentally,' said Alastair, 'my paternal grandmother, who was a concert pianist, studied music in Leipzig. She was deeply saddened by the two wars.'

'I'll go and make us a cup of tea,' said Mrs Warren, her mouth thinned into a line.

On the day of my departure Mrs Warren no doubt heaved a sigh and renewed her hopes that her son would one day bring home a nice Scottish lassie. Alastair saw me to the station. As we kissed good-bye, like friends, his eyes held a hint of sadness. But then he did not realize yet that I had saved our relationship. That in the coming years our affinity of spirit, our memories of fragile Tangermünde days, in which youth and integrity had proved themselves, would consolidate. That our friendship would ride smoothly through the Fourth and Fifth Age of Man, unafraid of the Sixth.

During the long journey south it was, however, not Shake-speare's Sonnet, nor the balancing of my emotional account, which gave me food for thought, but the information which Alastair had solicitously withheld from his German guest until the coach door was shut and I was leaning out of the window.

'I'm sorry, Marianne, if you found my mother a trifle . . . reserved at times. You see, my father was wounded three times and gassed twice during the First War. It affected his health. He died soon after I joined the Army.'

Shortly after my return to Oxford I was transferred to the Slade Isolation Hospital at Cowley, where an acute shortage of kitchen staff had arisen.

The 'Slade' formed a sprawling complex, consisting of a solid two-storey main building fronted by a parade of sycamore trees and backed by several isolation units and prefabricated staff huts. For two weeks I worked in the kitchen, scullery and nurses'

dining-room. I had my own small room in the resident domestics'
hut, where the walls seemed to be made of cardboard, doors and
windows jammed and water ran moodily from taps, not to speak
of the plumbing which would send orchestrated gurling, burping
and hissing noises throughout the fragile structure every time
anyone as much as looked at a cracked wash-basin, dirt-rimmed
bath or shaky toilet seat. Not that the domestics' dining-room-
cum-sitting-room, in which three grey-haired, long-serving Irish
maids set the rules, extended a welcome, or offered communication of the uplifting or heart-warming kind.

Alma, Maud and Dorothy, nicknamed 'Dot', had come to the
Slade long before the war. The hospital had become their home,
the sitting-room their sanctuary, colloquium, emotional chapel
and spa. Here they smoked, knitted, listened to light music and
comedy programmes on radio and kept up an interminable chatter
about the global events of their working day.

Needless to say, my appearance on the scene upset the finely
attuned equilibrium of their lives. For tall, slim and brunette,
educated to Abitur level, and intent on pushing my mind further
into the higher stratas of learning, I must have crashed into their
trefoil community like a football into a bed of tulips. The fact that
I was caught reading 'real' books, even poetry, and one afternoon
was glued to the radio, listening to a Mozart piano concerto,
quickly sealed my fate. I was an intruder, and a German one to
boot. Why, even my eating habits were different. I did not slurp or
talk with my mouth full, nor hold knife and fork like flagpoles
while I was chewing. It was manifestly clear: with the whiff of
another world I had brought a sense of unrest and insecurity into
their parlour, and the only way in which they felt they could deal
with such confrontation was by pointedly switching off a
Divertimento or an operatic aria in favour of *Mrs Dale's Diary* or
music-hall jokes. And, of course, the stranger in the midst could
always be sublimely ignored, except for requests to pass the salt or
the tomato ketchup at table.

Both Alma, who giggled and read comics, and Maud, a sour-
faced woman who would faithfully recount every word she had
exchanged with cook in their daily round of arguments, were
subservient to Dot. Stunted in growth, afflicted with a club-foot
and the suggestion of a hump, poor Dot suffered from short-
comings that had shaped her personality and found expression on

her crumpled, unsmiling face – a compound of lifelong frustrations, a dislike for mirrors and for anything likely to rock her
world in which she had secured herself a modicum of prestige.
Despite her physical disadvantages she always held her head as
high as her job as Matron's personal maid demanded, a distinction
of office which had automatically made her the major-domo of the
hospital domestics. Her word was law among the lower ranks.
Safe in the exclusive knowledge of how Matron liked her trays
laid, her meals served and her bed made, she would limp tirelessly
up and down the stairs, commuting between her lady's quarters,
the kitchen and her own pantry. Rumour would have it that no
magical cloth, cleaning or polishing agent could produce a more
dazzling shine on Matron's brass and silver, her parquet floor or
bathroom fittings. Over the years, in a position which gave her
the status she desperately needed to compensate for her physical
deformities, the humble, humdrum challenges of her job had
become Dot's way of life.

It was I who, assisted by a cruel fate and a sober-headed
Matron, had to deal her a most uncharitable blow.

On cleaning Matron's window one day, or slipping on her
super-polished floors – the exact cause of the accident was never
fully established – Dot broke her right arm and was henceforth
condemned to the boredom and physical restrictions of those
encumbered with a plaster cast. Speculations: How does one
replace the 'irreplaceable' Dot? Who would have the honour of
stepping, if temporarily, into her shoes?

Matron, used to the speedy and practical decisions of her
profession, soon provided the answer and restored first floor
routine, by appointing me her 'acting' maid.

The news wreaked havoc in the domestics' quarters. For not only
had I been promoted over the heads of such Slade loyals as Alma and
Maud, which was surely an injustice in itself, but I was a bloody
foreigner whose preoccupation with books, but most pointedly the
reading of *The Times*, suggested leanings not compatible with
domestic service. Surely, so whispers and piqued faces asserted, in
attending to Matron's needs the likes of me could not possibly
achieve excellence, nor serve her with Dot-like devotion.

I took matters in hand by questioning the reluctant invalid with
ambassadorial diplomacy about the laying of Matron's tray, her
meal-times and the time-span between each course to be carried up

to her room. I probed for the latter's idiosyncrasies and gave up when Dot's all too vague definitions of her former duties indicated that an imperfect initiation would hopefully dig my grave before long. Common sense and Matron's brief directives helped me cope. A week later I was still in my job. And now the cook had a ready smile for me; Maureen, the kitchen-hand showed me family photographs and the new scullery-maid came little short of addressing me as 'Miss'. Not to be outdone, my three Irish malcontents now muttered a 'Good morning' in my direction, and one afternoon sat through a whole hour of symphonic music without retuning the radio to their own tastes.

As the weeks wore on I found myself getting restless in a job in which I had to polish gleaming objects and surfaces to which even the sun could not have added further sparkle, and where dust had had no time to settle. In vain I looked for inspiration in the daily ritual of taking matron's lunch and dinner to her lounge, course by course, from soup to coffee, each trip a trayload up a flight of stairs and along a corridor. And there was something faintly repulsive in airing and making Matron's bed, in becoming an intruder into the intimate eiderdown zone of a lone, unspoused body, and a bathroom where the careless traces of talcum powder on the floor shamelessly evoked images of ageing folds of flesh being dabbed with Mornay Talc.

The days were dragging, lacking vital spark. One day, having engaged me in furtive conversation on the nurses' home corridor, a German student nurse, on hearing footsteps approaching, told me that she was not supposed to communicate with a member of the domestic staff.

'*Tut mir leid*'[1], she said, and whipped back into her room. I swallowed my humiliation, washed down with two mugs of tea my anger at a hospital rule which, like barbed wire, separated two working camps indiscriminately, bent only on keeping an inter-house cast system *in situ*. The lowliness of my status finally stunned me into the admission, '*Du musst dein Leben ändern*'[2].

The turning-point came when I received my examination results. I was jubilant. A 'Lower Two', a better result than I had expected. And I knew that the Diploma was more than something to frame or

---

1 'I'm sorry'
2 'You must change your life' (Rilke, New Poems) (Ernst Wiechert, *Das Einfache Leben*)

boost my morale. For my studies had broadened my vision, increased my vocabulary and sharpened my critical faculties. They had also, perhaps more than anything else, given me a thirst for literature and the seemingly infinite breadth of the English language as a vehicle for expression and comprehension. At the same time I realized that my 'little learning' would soon turn into an impediment a job which was mentally undemanding, and in which I might have been better off not to have tasted the 'Pierian spring where shallow draughts intoxicate the brain'. And the more I pondered my position, the more determined I grew to effect a change.

But there was no way in which to circumvent facts: Entrance to élitist Oxford University and other British universities, however coveted, was still closed to German nationals, until such a time as the West German university system re-established itself, complete with matriculation criteria, and the Deutschmark became an acceptable tender. Anyway, from where would the fees come? My father was dead, my mother earning a meagre living, and of my grandmother's estate, whatever capital had survived in the bank crash in twenty-three, had been spent on black market food during the hungry years. Besides, so soon after the war, even God was bound to have run out of miracles. Facts, unshakable, non-manipulable, to which I knew the wise person bows.

At the Labour Office they did not mince their words. I was German. I was over here on a contract. But then, ah, a loophole. What did I think of going into nursing? One of the requisites was a good standard of education. They needed girls like me, quick on the uptake, physically strong, neat in appearance. My stay in this country could be extended . . .

I saw myself in a white cap and crisp uniform – a white angel administering to grateful patients, and performing jobs that required skill and knowledge.

I decided to become a nurse.

Then came the rub.

'The only vacancy we have at the moment is for a nursing auxiliary at the Warnford Mental Hospital,' said the lady. They're desperately short of nurses. They'd welcome you with open arms.

The imagery was appealing. I accepted.

Two days before I was due to commence work at the Warnford, fed up with late autumn winds rattling the latch on my window and whistling through the corridor as through Pan's pipes, I went into town to see a film.

The Ritz Cinema was showing *The Snake Pit*, and long queues suggested that it was a film worth viewing. I got one of the last tickets, counted my pennies for an ice-cream and sat back in happy anticipation of an evening's entertainment. As it was, I had no idea what I was letting myself in for, nor that the film would make me doubt the wisdom of my decision to enter mental nursing. For no advance publicity of its disturbing content had reached the domestic quarters at the Slade, where listening to the news on radio smacked of intellectual arrogance, and nothing short of a national disaster or a happy royal event would have disturbed the aura of placidity.

Set against the background of an overcrowded American State Hospital, the film painted a grim, realistic picture of mental illness and some methods of treatment. Of violence forcibly constrained, disturbed minds drugged into docility, and the complete loss of reason and human dignity shut firmly away in wards that evoked images of Dante's Hell. It portrayed nurses whose sensibilities had been blunted through overwork and shortage of facilities, if not by years of exposure to the grey and dark labyrinths of sick minds. Seemingly forever locking and unlocking doors, they resembled prison wardresses. And what image of insanity at its rawest could the film-makers have conveyed to the viewer more strikingly, more nauseatingly and, indeed, more frighteningly, than a pit filled with snakes, wriggling, coiling, entwining?

I knew little about mental illness and mental hospitals. Why, to the casual observer, Hitler's Germany had been a country without asylums, tucked away in remote areas as they were. Their inmates and selfless carers had never made the news. Now, with hindsight, I knew that racial purists had 'murdered' legions of mentally-handicapped people, the freaks of nature, they said, who did not fit into the Nazi concept of German mental and physical health, and thus had no right to live. Yet I was not deaf to the timid voice inside me, which argued that the induction of a painless death might be an act of compassion, where the incurably insane, chained to their own hell, were not drawing one iota of quality from life.

But then another voice dissented: 'Thou shall not kill!'

3

The Snake Pit

The hospital stood in several acres of parkland and gardens, its wards separated from the compact two-storey nurses' home by a lawn the size of a cricket pitch, and by flower beds in which November was taking its toll among the chrysanthemums.

My room faced the park and was pleasantly furnished in light oak. A dressing table, a sturdy wardrobe, an armchair, pretty curtains on the windows and reading lamps all reflected my rise in the hospital world.

To my surprise I found that in the absence of a rigid hierarchical nursing structure at the Warnford, trained staff, student nurses and auxiliaries enjoyed the same privileges.

Nowhere was this more evident than in the beautiful, wood-panelled staff dining-room where, among silver, hot plates, dainty place mats and flowers, staff seated themselves around the banquet-sized mahogany table irrespective of rank and seniority. And nothing drove home the reversal of roles more pointedly than a maid serving me breakfast in bed on my days off. The luxury of it! And how such privilege cuddled my ego.

The sudden ascent from the lowest rung of the hospital ladder was indeed a striking one, but it did not take long before I felt comfortable in my new environment. And perhaps I would also have warmed to my new job if the initiation of duties had not taken place on the Female Psycho-Geriatric Ward. Or if I had known more about the working of the human mind than Freudian theories on the Id and the Ego. If I had known how the paths of reason may be twisted, blocked or lying fallow; how dignity may be divested as easily as a night shirt, and sanity, once it has deserted its host, leave behind nothing but a body shell.

I had no idea what awaited me. I had never been a patient or a visitor in a large hospital ward, nor had I ever nursed anyone. Now, on my first morning, I was thrown in at the proverbial deep end, head first.

This is where they made their mistake. Whether through oversight or an acute staff shortage that day, it was the kind of blunder which in newcomers to mental nursing might well raise second thoughts about their chosen profession and plunge sensitive novices like myself into a state of 'nerves'.

Senile Dementia reigned supremely in Female Three – the pit of wasted, uncoordinated minds, the testing ground of the caring spirit and of utter committal. Here, duties were basic, confined to washing bodies, cleaning up bodies, feeding bodies, placing bodies on bedpans and distributing paraldehyde to unmanageable patients. As part of a small team of nurses, who did not stand on their stripes of seniority, I also helped to make beds, wiped up urine, scraped faecal matter off the walls and spit off my apron. But no cotton wool could plug my ears and shield me against the inmates' constant babbling, screaming, shrieking, giggling and repetitive monologues. In Female Three, I thought, it was hard to hold on to one's own sanity.

Off duty there was little respite for me, as images increasingly assailed my inner eye, unwilling to be side-tracked by such diversionary activities as reading, listening to the radio or washing my hair or undies. From Day One, nightmares plagued me, only to find new nourishment on the ward next morning. But how to exorcize grimaces, or stares fixed to the core of an alien world? How to forget about limbs wriggling like snakes or performing queer antics; hands playing with excreta and nightgowned ghostlike figures lurching through bedspaces with infantile smiles?

Perhaps I would have managed in time to demarcate reality, perhaps my sensibility would have weathered its visual and aural affront if it had not been for Mrs F., a tiny lady, all skin and bones and pleading eyes.

'Dearie, give me another cup of tea!' she would wail from

her bed, minute after minute, every waking hour of the day, and no matter how many sips of tea she had. Why another cup of tea? I asked myself. Why constantly articulate one and the same request, just as if her mind had got stuck at a moment in time when she had thirsted for another cup of the brew?

At the end of the second week, I came off duty, dazed, tears running down my cheeks. For whatever sleep I had snatched since my arrival at the Warnford had not been restorative, not against the jungle of images in which my mind was entrapped, not against that entreating voice – the soundtrack to my nightmares: 'Dearie, give me another cup of tea!'

Matron caught my crumpled self in the corridor.

'Come and see me in my office, nurse!'

And later, 'I'm sorry that Female Three appears to be too much for you. What I want you to do is to take the rest of the morning off. Have a good sleep, then go for a walk. Tomorrow, report to Female Four. You might find the going a little easier there. If you'd like, I could arrange for you to attend certain lectures. They would give you a better insight into mental illness and modern therapy. During the last two decades some revolutionary changes have been made in the treatment of schizophrenia, depression and certain psychoses. I know, nurse, you'll get a grip on yourself. You've been doing well so far, I hear. I wouldn't like to lose you.'

Her smile followed me to the door.

I washed my face, took a bus into town and walked down St Aldgates to Folly Bridge, and down the footpath by the river.

It was cold and unseasonally calm, which gave the river a leaden sheen and somnolent quality, while in the absence of craft the duck population enjoyed the freedom of a mid-stream swim. A film of ice had formed on puddles and Christ Church stood pale in the frosty light. I walked briskly, my mind shedding troublesome images and replacing them with peaceful river views.

On my way back I called at Bishop King's Palace. Linde was expecting her first baby early in the new year, and she proudly exhibited her rounded belly.

I thought there was nothing like nature, or the sight of expectant motherhood, to restore equilibrium. And what could put back the spark into one more speedily and more effectively than 'a nice cup' of English tea and a thick slice of Dundee cake served in front of an open fire?

On Female Four I became a prison wardress and round-the-clock watcher.

'Here are your keys, nurse,' said the staff nurse, 'guard them with your life! Always keep the ward locked. And the bathroom door. And the various cabinets. Hang on to your scissors. Never put them down. The same goes for your pen. And never lose sight of a patient. They're all potentially dangerous – to us, to their fellow inmates, to themselves. You see, some of them are suicidal. They'll try anything to end their lives. Some are homicidal. You never know when, how and whom they'll attack. Very clever they are. You'd think their one aim in life is to outwit you. That's why we have no knives, forks or glasses on the ward, nor any objects that could be used as weapons. Keep a special eye on Minnie, she's just waiting to stick something into you. So, watch, watch, watch! Oh, and I'd better warn you, Helen, over there, a schizo, can be quite abusive with her tongue.'

As the nurse took me round the bright, airy ward, outlining the patients' histories, I felt a wide avenue of new experience opening up for me.

Most of the patients were up and dressed during the day, unless undergoing special treatment. Subject to notoriously unpredictable and impulsive behaviour, the schizophrenics might be brooding for days,. before exploding into house-wives' chatter, highbrow talk or dramatic monologues, each depend-ing on her education or career background. Listless suicidals might erupt into a frenzied restlessness. For days or weeks, a homicidal patient might hide her murderous intentions behind a smile, her complaisant or angelic manner mocking sanity – a dangerous state likely to lure an inexperienced nurse into relaxing her vigilance. And there was Mrs B., a manic depressive, whose total unresponsive-ness had created a miasma of living death around her bed.

Deep in the catatonic vale of her illness, she was lying with her face turned towards the wall and her knees drawn up, deaf to the goings-on around her, her mouth closed to the spoon that tried to feed her, her body apathetic towards the cloth that washed her.

The responsiveness of some patients either to conversation or to the various treatments at which I assisted, added interest to the ward routine, while in-house lectures opened my mind to the aetiology of mental disease. Soon it became clear to me that the patients' real prison was their illness, not a locked ward.

I was fascinated by ink blot tests in which patients were required to translate to the doctor their definitions of a series of black blotches – a popular diagnostic aid to discover a homicidal potential or provide information about the kind of phantoms that inhabited a disturbed mind. Inevitably, my own imagination took part in the 'game'. But whereas I might see a starfish, a spider's web or an exotic flower in a bizarre shape, one patient might define it as a 'blood stain', or the 'spill of a poisonous liquid', another as 'a tarantula ready to strike', a third as 'evil embodied, tentacled'.

I gritted my teeth at the sight of strapped bodies injected with the muscle relaxant curare and electrically shocked into convulsive rigidity, to stimulate depressed brain areas – a therapy which often produced amazing results. I witnessed insulin shock treatment. For hours I would sit at the bedside of a schizophrenic patient in whom a hypoglycaemic coma had been induced, monitoring a seemingly lifeless body, until consciousness was restored by glucose drip feed or insulin injections.

Electrodes, injections, diagnostic tests, charts. Eyes trained on patients' behaviour. A bunch of keys giving a sense of power. Nakedness in the bath tub, watched through a window in the door. No chances taken. Emotions left behind at the ward door. Personal detachment, to delineate on-duty and off-duty spheres, but leaving an essential part in me unstirred, untouched.

It was not until Mrs B. turned away from the wall one morning and called me over, that I crossed the boundary of self-enforced emotional anaesthesia.

'Nurse, could you please come and sit on my bed for a minute?' she asked, groping for my hand. And as she slowly returned into a brighter, sharply defined world, I felt something mellowing inside me. With the warmth of my palm, and for a prayer-length of unclinical attention, I was giving of myself, of my own strength and humanity. Perhaps, I mused many years later, it was in these silent moments that a sense of caring was born.

'Thank you, nurse,' said Mrs B, when she finally let go of my hand, the dawn of a smile on her face, 'Do you think there's the chance of a cup of tea?'

The weathermen called 17 January 1950 the coldest day of the century, but one which bore the good tidings that rationing would soon end. It was the day I went on night duty.

In its dim, bluish light the Male Psycho-Geriatric Ward offered experiences of the weird kind. In sixteen side-boarded beds inmates slept a drugged sleep, hallucinated or lay wide-eyed and alarmingly awake. Male Three was also the home of several paranoics, and it was here that I met Napoleon, Caesar and Hitler.

Even during the night these patients were often unable to shake off the ghosts they inhabited, and paraldehyde might sometimes have the effect of making one or the other climb out of bed, taking his seignorial dreams through the ward, strutting, issuing commands or bestowing honours on invisible worthies.

Nowhere rang a Shakespearian truth more true than on Male Three, where the heads that wore crowns – whether imperial, made of laurels or consisting of no more than a peaked brown cap with the swastika emblem – lay uneasy.

Being reasonably conversant with the reigns of famous or infamous potentates, it was easy for me to humour a nocturnal rambler and coax him back to bed. After all, history had chronicled most explicitly the lives and feats, the battles, crimes and delusions of grandeur of the respective statesman, emperor and dictator, and each in his time had been a willing receptacle for homage.

Some nights started off quietly enough, with the patients' adenoidal sounds likely to lull me into a false sense of security and the small hours ahead looming like a passage through the Valley of Eternal Night. However, the spotting of an empty bed, vague sounds tumbling out of a dark corner, or the sly lurch of a night-gowned figure towards my desk, would release instant adrenaline and put me on guard, especially just before dawn, when my eye-lids felt heavy and mental functions were at an ebb.

'Don't leave it too late,' the Sister had warned me when I first went 'on nights'. 'That's what the red button on your desk is for. Press it when you think you need help.'

But though my finger had frequently hovered over the 'Danger' button, I had pressed it only once, when Napoleon, having marched on his spindly legs to the ward door, shouting '*Vive la France!*', tried to kick it open with his bare feet, in order to lead his troops into battle, and when he threatened to have me beheaded on the spot if I did not unlock the 'Gate of Paris' immediately.

When I came off night-duty I found myself doing basic early morning or evening duties on a single-room tract of the Female Psycho-Contained Ward, and spending the rest of my day-time shift in a verandah-type lounge which nurses euphemistically called the 'Observatory', and which patients, according to their background or leanings, had named the 'Greenhouse' or 'Winter garden'.

On Female V most patients were ambulatory. Some were sedated, which eased their handling whilst granting them in between pills a pseudo-peace of mind, if not a slender quality of life. Others already stabilized, or with their intelligence little impaired, welcomed any distraction and the various means of occupational ward therapy on offer.

The long windows of the lounge admitted broad shafts of light and the first green tints of spring. Evergreen pot plants, a moss-green carpet and green-patterned chair and settee covers exuded warmth and a visual serenity that could not fail to soothe receptive areas of the patients' minds.

Burrowed deeply into chairs and settees, some were dozing or chatting, others were strolling around or trying to cope with jig-saw puzzles, dominoes or women's magazines. One foursome, to whom nurses referred as the 'four-leaf clover', spent each afternoon at a card table, playing bridge. At a glance, the uninitiated observer might have taken the scene for the lounge of an English residential seaside hotel.

My Observatory duties were light. They included the locking and unlocking of the door, escorting patients to the toilet and engaging them in conversation, not forgetting to give credit whenever an iota of credit was due, and encouragement where a patient had a good chance to move towards a more stable behavioural pattern. Ostensibly, I was a lounge companion, friend, adviser and confidante, and only the locked door and my rattling bunch of keys singled me out as an overseer. Strange nurse-patient relationships developed in such enforced proximity, often lasting no longer than a few hours or, at most, a day or two. In the morning, a patient might relate to me her past life of sin, piety or feats worthy of a Joan of Arc; she might bare her family history, confide her innermost desires. Yet, back on my afternoon shift, or next morning, she might not remember her divulgences, nor even my face.

'Are you new here, nurse? What's your name?'

Some patients liked to pay compliments.

'You have such lovely hair.'

One lady never ceased to show off her genteel upbringing. Holding her head high and her shoulders squared, she moved around the room like a dowager. Her accent was clipped, her tone of voice suggested servants at home, and in the way she took her afternoon tea, she might have been in a ducal drawing-room, her mug a cup made of the finest porcelain.

There were the bridge players who would endlessly argue over a wrongly-played trump or the wisdom of bidding 'no trump' over 'one spade'. One player, a former actress and opium addict, was the queen of the bridge table. Articulate, and with the Thespian's razor-sharp pronunciation, she held her foursome tightly together. Widely travelled, she also made a good conversationalist. The places she had been, the great actors she had partnered on stage, the famous people she had met! . . .

Where did truth end and fantasy begin I wondered.

Outside, spring had exploded, and on fine days I now took patients for a walk in the walled garden, one at a time. Hospital rules were strict and vigilance a prime part of a nurse's duties. Yet it was sometimes easy to forget that a patient, with whom I was strolling along the gravel path, arm in arm, admiring the daffodils or watching chaffinches stealing crumbs from under the beaks of blackbirds, was sporadically divorced from reality or wholly living in a world of make-believe. Not infrequently, their mental states might shift between a massive oak on one end of the garden and a budding rhododendron bush on the other. I found such erratic pattern, and my own inability to plumb the prevailing mental condition of a patient, most unnerving. For hard as I tried, my own powers proved grossly inadequate.

'Use your instinct, nurse,' said the Sister. 'Keep the doors locked at all times. Walk with the patients, talk to them, humour them, let the joy of spring into their minds, but above all keep your eyes open. Patients on Female Five may no longer be dangerous to us or to themselves, but we never know what trick a sick mind might play, what foolish things it might get up to. She pointed to the beanstalk of a woman who was watering the pot plants in the lounge.

'Jackie is no risk. You can let her out alone into the corridor and dining-area. She always lays the table and helps with meals. Ever since she's had her frontal lobectomy she's very docile, very quiet, doing everything at half her former pace. Perhaps in a few months she'll be ready for a life outside.'

To encourage 'normal' social behaviour, a Social was held for selected patients every fortnight. There was music and dancing in a hall of manorial proportions, followed by tea and cake. Doctors and nurses danced with the patients, the patients with each other. For an hour a muted fair-ground mood prevailed, bringing smiles to patients' faces and, so therapists hoped, a flicker of sunshine into their lives. Two nurses put it more succinctly.

'The music eases mental tension.'

'The dancing gives their brains a shake-up.'

Off they went to join hands with the patients for a 'Hokey-Cokey'.

The first tulips were out when the life I had made for myself at the Warnford collapsed quietly.

The morning had started auspiciously enough. Someone, it

was found, had mutilated the proud rubber plant in the lounge, neatly clipping the tip off each leaf. An enquiry into this heinous crime was still under way, with fingernails being inspected for sharp edges and evidence of chlorophyll, when Mrs P., a normally sedate elderly lady, who had been working at the jig-saw puzzle of a farm-yard, suddenly thrashed her fists in frustration through the incomplete picture, sending fragments of grazing cows flying.

In another corner of the lounge, a grey-haired, inconspicuous patient, who seldom spoke, and who had never been inconti-nent before, waved me towards her, wistfully pointing to her 'accident' which had soaked her clothes and the armchair. And as if this was not enough in the way of minor interruptions, the actress gave her partner a furious look in mid-game, threw her cards on the table and vociferously expressed her indignation.

'How could you bid two hearts when you have a solid rubber, you fool?'

She leapt up and went to the window, opened it and pressed her face against the bars. A scent of Daphne and awaking soil drifted into the room. Behind her, the remaining players studied their cards.

'It's spring-time,' the actress stated, raising her husky voice one melodious decibel, 'the only pretty ring-time, when birds do sing, hey ding a ding ding. Sweet lovers love the spring.' And after a pause, 'How bright the sun is shining today!'

She turned sharply. And now I watched the curtain going up and Julia taking the stage – a middle-aged *ingénue* across whose face a tractor seemed to have cut deep ruts. Her hands reached into the room towards her invisible lover.

'O Romeo, Romeo! Wherefore art thou, Romeo?' she exclaimed, with perfect diction and heart-rendering intonation. Closing her eyes, she retreated into a distant sensual darkness. 'Come, gentle night, come loving, black-brow'd night/give me my Romeo; and when I shall die/Take him and cut his heart out in little stars . . . '

But she had no audience in her fellow-patients who, ignoring the actress' transformation, continued their dozing and chat-ting, while her bridge-partners, possibly used to dramatic outbursts in mid-play, threw in their hands and discussed the possibility of another game or two, to make a rubber. I was the only listener to Julia's soliloquy, and when she had ended my applause rang stiffly through the room. With an expert wave of her hand, the lone performer graciously acknowledged my appreciation. Then, the interlude over, and the final curtain lowered, she went back to the table where card shuffling was in progress.

'Who's dealing?' she asked airily.

I felt something rising from my chest, reaching my throat, constricting it.

The Labour Exchange invited the next logical step.

'I'd like to train as a general nurse,' I said.

The Clerk tested my motivation and busied herself with files.

'We have a vacancy at King Edward VII Hospital at Windsor,' she said. 'Their next Preliminary Training Course will start in May, in Bray Court, near Maidenhead. I'll make the necessary arrangements to have your Labour Permit extended.'

Back at the Warnford, the Matron tried to persuade me to stay on and acquire full mental nursing qualifications.

'We need nurses like yourself,' she said, 'conscientious, committed, eager to learn . . . '

I found it difficult to counter her arguments, to verbalize the dichotomy inside me. I knew I genuinely wanted to help sick people, not just to play a bedside angel. Yet, deep down, I was clamouring for an atmosphere of sanity in which patients visibly responded to medical and nursing care, and rewarded staff with smiles and the rising bloom of returning health. Stubbornly, my mind repelled the thought of death being laid out under white sheets; it refused to project images of blood, pus and horrific wounds. Perhaps there was a grain of naivety in my line of reasoning, if not selfishness. Perhaps my decision to change my working environment stemmed from my own vulnerability which, for months, like a wind harp, had been recording the oscillations of alienated minds or, where cerebral Nemesis had taken place, their terminal silence.

In retrospect, my departure from the Warnford looked more like an act of survival.

4

Skeleton, leeches and blancmange

Bray Court, a rambling Victorian mansion, stood in several acres of gardens. A screen of flaming rhododendron bushes hid ground long given over to nature, and a closely-trimmed lawn bordered on a jungle of weeds. Built by a member of a Scotch whisky family at the turn of the century, it featured 365 windows – one for every day of the year – an architectural idiosyncracy which, in the days to come, would have its new occupants madly counting and recounting.

In World War I the Haigs had moved out to make room for the wounded. By 1928, the mansion had changed occupants several times, before opening as the Bray Court School for Boys.

'They say, Gloria Vanderbilt once lived here,' said the Junior Sister Tutor, as she took the new intake of trainee nurses on a tour of the house. 'It also served as a hotel and country club, and as a home for refugee children from the Spanish Civil War. In World War II the government used it for offices, while after the war, and before King Edward VII Hospital acquired it for its Preliminary Nursing School, it housed the Merchant Navy's cadet training centre.'

Although the proverbial tooth of time had visibly been gnawing at the formidable mansion, the spacious, high-ceilinged rooms still bore witness to former manorial grandeur. In its wood-panelled Hall, light streamed through cathedral-like windows, to rest on the high polish of two king-sized dinner-tables. Effortlessly, my imagination reached back in time, evoking a hunting-feast, with goblets raised for toasts, husky merriment and servants floating into the Hall, carrying silver platters of roast game of pheasants garnished like trophies . . .

'This is the Hall,' said the Sister. And, pointing to two miniscule jars on each place mat, 'They contain your weekly butter and sugar rations.'

73

Once rooms had been allocated, uniforms and time-tables issued, the Senior Sister Tutor delivered her welcoming address which, seasoned with rules and the sweet-sour smiles of authority, presaged a sense of iron hospital discipline. Young faces narrowed. But only temporarily, for on this our first day in a nurse's uniform we were all bursting with Florence Nightingale spirit, if not with an overwhelming curiosity for the ebb and flow of hospital life.

I was not the only German at Bray Court. Lotte, daughter of a Professor of Surgery, and a qualified physiotherapist, and Trudi, professing to a humbler background, had both been recruited in Germany for training as student nurses. They could not have been more different in appearance and character.

Blond, bovine-faced Trudi lacked Lotte's agility of mind and manners, an ease that often comes with growing up in an academic household and within a social class accorded great respect in title and rank-conscious Germany. A smile never dwelt long enough on Trudi's face to invite response, and being too stiff and guarded it seldom extended to uninhibited laughter. Built like a Valkyrie – the national socialist image of German womanhood – her broad back and shoulders made it clear that they would shield her from anything hostile to her nature and aspirations.

In contrast, brunette, impish-faced Lotte, whose volubility was easy to tolerate, was endowed with an ubiquitous sense of humour, and her propensity for turning the most pedestrian remark into jokes worthy of contagious laughter, often had me doubling up like a teenager, and even Trudi emitting sounds of levity.

Trudi possessed a working knowledge of English acquired during the first two years of British occupation. Not so Lotte, who confessed to a dismally poor English vocabulary, and to speculations that she had been selected solely on the strength of her career-based knowledge of anatomy and physiology. And since she was terrified of slipping into one of the many potholes of the English language, she clung to Trudi for support in all matters of communication not related to bones and muscles, a position which Trudi clearly enjoyed.

The two girls shared a room. They sat next to each other in the class-room, at table and in the lounge, which in no time had their English colleagues nicknaming them 'The Heavenly Twins'. Inevitably, unaware of the dangers of translating some English words all too literally, Lotte learnt one day that the addition of an 's' to a noun does not always make for the plural, but for a different meaning, and that sometimes, if used with a certain verb, such a combination can form a pitfall for the foreigner.

Morning figures were descending the broad staircase, one day, yawning, closing a last dress button or steadying a cap with a hair clip.

'Come on, Lotte,' Trudi shouted from the landing.

Through the open bedroom door Lotte's baritone voice echoed down the stairs loud and clear:

'Just a minute, I'm just combing my hairs.'

Shrieks of laughter, merriment spreading to the breakfast tables. For days, Lotte's innocent slip provided a source of gleeful remarks:

'I say, where's Lotte? Is she still combing her hairs?'

'Why did you come over?' I asked the 'Twins' one day.

'Lots of reasons,' said Trudi, her starched expression making it clear that she did not wish to elaborate.

'After the currency reform I found myself without a job,' replied Lotte. 'Besides, in our family it was always part of one's education to spend a year or two abroad.'

Older than the 'Twins' by two years, and occupying a single room I found it difficult to add myself as a 'third wheel' to their buggy. Only united in laughter, or in speaking German safely distanced from English ears, did we form a trio.

A skeleton hanging on a stand, religiously shrouded when not used for teaching purposes, dominated the class-room, while a standard hospital bed, occupied by a papier-mâché patient, formed the focal point of the practical-nursing room.

Not unexpectedly, as the pressure of condensed study and cloistered life bore upon us, we were prone to directing irreverent remarks at these two inert objects for humorous relief or the temporary discharge of frustration.

For eleven weeks we swotted over anatomy and physiology. Lectures in Hygiene taught us about the control of flies and vermin, ventilation, sewage works, cross-infection and lice-infestation. In Cookery classes we learnt to prepare junket, beef tea, egg custard, blancmange and steamed fish. In Practical Nursing we were shown how to make a hospital bed envelope-style, with its bottom sheet tucked in at an angle of forty-five degrees, and counterpanes stretched tightly across the model's toes, sides draping parallel to the floor, which had me wondering about the patient's comfort. Other lessons: how to blanket-bath, give a warmed-up bedpan and wash a patient's hair; how to turn the administration of a soap and water enema through tube and funnel into an art, a procedure which a volunteer was asked to demonstrate on the model, by inserting a length of tubing into the appropriate orifice. A horrified Sister Tutor:

'Not that far, nurse! You're not doing a gastric lavage.'

And there was the mock-sponging of feverish patients, the preparation of kaoline poultices and, nauseatingly, the real-life application of blood-thirsty leeches which fortunately found papier-mâché of little appeal.

Discipline was strict, and during the week Bray Court felt like a nunnery. To be physically prepared for the long duty hours that awaited us on the wards, a gym instructress with the lean looks of a marathon runner and the voice of a drill sergeant lined us up on the lawn every morning before breakfast for exercises identical to the 'keep fit' regimen of school and Hitler Youth days. In the evenings we would sit around in the lounge, reading, knitting or crocheting, while the *Warsaw Concerto* or the *Mikado* were being massacred on scratched records.

Weekends brought freedom from morning drill, starched uniforms, black shoes and stockings, as well as from the communal lounge with its aura of harnessed femininity. They also brought experiences remembered for more than the intrinsic quality of warm summer days: walks through maturing fields or along the riverbank; boating on the calm waters of the Thames, over which the air seemed to stand still, and where, amid flower scent bearing down from riverside gardens, and undisturbed by passing craft, no other sound would steal into my heat-drowsy mood than the humming of insects, the placid action of my oars and the occasional wing-flapping of a playful duck. How reminiscent of a lake scene in Potsdam, years ago, treasured . . .

An episode, a bout of mid-summer madness, unforgotten for the intensity of feelings it aroused in me, soon tempered my attention in the classroom.

Thomas, a final-year law student, was the spitting image of John Lund, the Swedish film star. According to women's magazines, avidly read by my fellow-trainees, he was rated the current male screen idol. We met at the village cricket ground at the end of Saturday's play.

Eyes the colour of a South Sea lagoon, a smile unfastening female reserve, a smooth voice aiming for conquest.

'What's your name? Where do you come from? Do you like cricket? Will you have a drink with me?'

Cricketers, I thought, worked fast when it came to talking up a girl.

In the club-house, elbows anchored to the bar or standing in cocktail-party fashion, gentlemen dressed in white were conducting post-mortems on wickets and overs. As the afternoon lengthened, laughter lost its restraint, someone switched on the radio, a slow waltz turned the room into a dance hall.

'Come, let's have a dance.'

In Thomas's arms I feel the ground under my feet caving in and my bones turning to plasticine. When had I last been so magnificently aware of a man's propinquity, of masculinity oozing from his every pore?

And later, 'May I take you home?'

My chemistry is working overtime. I stumble over a stone, my tongue ties in a knot. I am a school-girl all over again, held in thraldom by her first date. Reality is Thomas's arm around my shoulder. It is, far too soon, his face, my throbbing pulse. Around us, crickets perform incidental music . . .

'May I see you again, Marianne?'

Further escapes from study and discipline to where summer magic embroils the senses. An after-dinner stroll down to the river, watching the water growing dark and losing the reflections of elm and willow trees. An afternoon on Monkey Island. Being ferried across in a punt by an old crony who had to be fetched from a nearby pub, and who instead of shillings and sixpences charged us two bottles of Lager for the return fare.

Our relationship was doomed from the start. Aching for love,

I had fallen in love, an easy victim to the mid-summer flutterings of the heart. Thomas, however, held romance in small esteem, and it took me several dates to realize that his intent and desires dwelt between his legs alone, and that 'to make love' was no more than an English euphemism for sex. But although I felt as if I were drowning in the sea of my longings, I remained impervious to his words of seduction, to endearments that came from lips and not, I sensed, from his heart. The old-fashioned code with which I had grown up and the more romantic concept of love I was still nursing, decided the issue for me.

Not surprisingly, my emotional turmoil lowered my perform-ance in the class-room. One day, asked to identify the skeleton's upper extremities, I connected the tibula to the shoulder joint, which, seen geographically, corresponded to Italy bordering on Norway. An indulgent Sister Tutor:

'Try again, nurse. Ever since the times of Adam . . . '

One evening, Thomas told me that he could not see me again. His vacations were coming to an end, bar examinations were looming ahead. And he did not hedge about the real reason for discontinuing our tug-of-war relationship.

'You're a sweet girl, Marianne, but such a romantic! I think you're looking for something in me I'm unable to give. I'll be honest with you: I'm afraid I'm a promiscuous man.'

I walked up the driveway, dying a little inside, but not feeling any wiser. What did he mean by being 'promiscuous'? I wondered, such adjective still missing from my English vocabulary.

At Bray Court I walked without a chip on my shoulder. The Sister Tutors, judging their students by their performances in the class-room, general demeanour and adherence to house rules, never labelled the German intake 'Nazis', whether directly or by inference. By the same token, our fellow nurses, most of whom were school-leavers and appallingly ignorant of the German scene, never referred to us as 'bloody Krauts'. And once they had got tired of staring at the children of the former Reich, and made sure that we had nothing in common with the Nazi monsters of screen and war-time propaganda, they tolerated us in their midst like freckles on their skin.

The beginning of August signalled written and practical

exams. Every candidate passed, even Lotte who had learnt whole text-book passages by heart and had compensated for her poor essay English with high marks in anatomy and physiology. And it was Lotte again who during her practical test sparked off a round of laughter. Asked by Sister Tutor where to put the poultice she had prepared for the imaginary Mr Smith, a patient suffering from bronchitis and a troublesome cough, Lotte pointed to the model's sexless chest, 'On his breasts, Sister.'

5

'Nurse!'

Windsor's King Edward VII Hospital was built in horse-shoe fashion, its thirty-two-bed wards and operating theatre overlooking a well-kept tennis court for senior staff at the rear. The main building was connected to the Nurses' Home by a corridor, the length of which was said effectively to space a nurse's mind from her day or night shift, if not necessarily from some bedside drama or gory theatre proceedings.

The Nurses' Home, a solid red brick building, faced a grassed area at the back and a tennis court in front. Three separate sitting-rooms, one each for student nurses, staff nurses and sisters, neatly separated grades. My room was cubicle-sized and functional, but books, photographs and pictures soon imparted a homely look. For here was to be my haven, a place where I would recharge my energy and digest whatever new experiences were lying in wait for me.

As one of the most junior members of the nursing hierarchy, I was forthwith assigned to the most menial ward tasks: emptying bedpans and sputum mugs, cleaning bedside lockers, rubber 'Macs' and dressing trolleys. In addition to giving patients a bed-bath and sterilizing dishes and instruments, I drew stomach fluid from patients on fractional test meals and, during visiting-time, rolled cotton wool into balls, and cut and folded gauze, to be packed into drums for sterilizing. If I was lucky, I was allowed to dispense Mist. Ipecacuhana, Cascara or Castor Oil. Bed-making took up much time, and each day before Matron's round, and before doors were opened to visitors, sheets and counterpanes were straightened, pillows plucked from behind a patient's head, to be shaken, even if nothing needed straightening or shaking.

As the weeks wore on, I was shown how to lay trolleys and trays for medical and surgical procedures, how to give penicillin and streptomycin injections, or premedications. And only experience taught the novice how to avoid causing misery to patients' backsides through barbed needles sterilized in a boiler and used over and over again.

Every morning nursing staff, consisting on average of one staff nurse and two or three student nurses for each shift, were called to Sister's room. Lined up in order of seniority, hands behind our backs, we listened to the ward report and were given assignments consummate with status and experience.

I soon learnt that the in-house hierarchy started at those line-ups, and woe betide a newcomer to the profession should she forget her place. Status consciousness was particularly prevalent among student nurses, none of whom seemed immune to the sweet smell of power over junior grades and often to the military-style flaunting of status as a tonic for a flaccid ego.

The privileges of status often bordered on the ludicrous, and they did not stop at the ward door. I admit that I frequently incurred a nurse's glowering look when, through sheer over-sight or the itch to rebel, I failed to let her pass through a door first, or stand aside for her on the stairways, even though her seniority might be as little as three months. However, my time came when another intake of student nurses arrived from the Preliminary Training School to take over as rock bottom juniors, thus elevating my own position by a degree.

Another unwritten rule not to be broken by junior staff with impunity reigned in the student nurses' sitting-room. Here, a first-year nurse was not expected to lay claim to armchairs closest to the electric fire or the radio, and during afternoon tea any junior not wanting to be lumbered with the most boring, most malodorous or nauseating tasks on her next shift, would wait patiently until 'the higher orders' had helped themselves to tea and, of course, to all the chocolate Digestives.

While the befriending of nurses senior by more than one year was frowned upon, any direct dealings with House Officers, Registrars or – heavens forbid – with Consultants, the hospital's deities, would court disaster. The rule was clear: approached by doctors on nursing or clinical procedures, a junior nurse would call her senior who, in turn would either summon the staff nurse or the sister to attend to the matter.

One particular lesson I learnt the hard way in First Year was that to advance my own theories, or to question a decision of the higher nursing ranks, was asking for trouble. For it was easy for them to find a discrepancy in my weekly laundry count ('Do it again, nurse!') or to allocate jobs to me no one else wanted to do.

Being part of the block system, which had come into operation under the new National Health Plan, we worked weekly shifts totalling forty-eight hours. During the first few months I was always too exhausted at the end of a shift to go out or socialize, and not even the half mile of corridor back to my room managed to expunge the impressions which had been bombarding my mind – the faces of disease and death, the ugliness of a wound, the horror of a bedsore eating into bone and the smells, some of which Lucifer seemed to have manufactured in his own laboratory.

Gradually, time balanced the scale, and I came to see the happier side of the picture: patients heaving themselves out of their illness, smiling, wounds healing, colour returning to cheeks and gratitude being expressed through handshakes and Cadbury chocolates. And I began to recognize my own small role in the scheme of things, if not the fact that, coming off duty, I could always wash my hands or take a shower, stock up with fresh air, play tennis or shut my door firmly behind the day's work.

There were limits, however, to the extent and quality of my leisure time. Remuneration for first-year toils – after deduction of board and lodgings and superannuation – came to barely six pounds a month, just enough for a weekly cinema visit, chocolates and a packet of Woodbines – a smoke being considered as a 'sophisticated' relaxant and 'very adult', even if one derived little pleasure from it. Out of this princely sum I also had to pay the cobbler for renewing ward-worn heels and replace laddered black stockings.

One of the privileges I enjoyed as a member of the hospital's nursing staff were the complimentary tickets issued by the Theatre Royal for matinées or stand-by nights.

Afternoon performances had little in common with matinées in Berlin, as I remembered them before total war brought stage curtains down in Germany. Then, ladies wore an afternoon dress and left their coats and furs in cloak-rooms, and during the performance theatre-goers did not dare to impose a whisper or the rattling of toffee-paper on actors and their fellow-audience.

In contrast, the matinée atmosphere at the Royal was charged with uninhibited tea-time pleasure. Matrons, their shopping stored under their seats, watched the happenings on stage in hats and coats. They laughed with abandon or shared the wit or drama of a scene with their neighbours. During the interval, the stalls turned into a tea-party. Trays with cakes, biscuits and tea were handed along the rows, and often, by the time the curtain rose again, these were still being collected, the tinkling of cups and saucers forming an unlikely background to an actor's entrance.

Skilled in the art of adaption, I soon fitted into a hospital framework bonded by hard work, rules and discipline, and run with great attention to the laws of hierarchy. The regimentation of student nurses and other resident staff below the rank of sister by a Home Sister and Domestic Supervisor did little, however, to uphold enthusiasm for a career in which returns were measured in job satisfaction alone, and in terms of time, money and outside interests gave young healthy women a raw deal.

Home Rule Number One decreed that all student nurses were required to be in by ten pm, when doors were locked. 'Lights out' was at eleven pm. This was to ensure that nurses would wake up next morning refreshed, facing their patients without yawns and their work without a trace of fatigue. Religiously, at the stroke of eleven, clicking heels would warn of the approach of one of the guardians of virtue and early slumber, and lights, visible through a glass panel over each bedroom door, would switch off obediently – at least until the sound of footsteps had died away.

But where a rule deprives sweethearts of the bewitching hour or the Last Dance, a system designed for its circumvention will be found. At King Edward's, the formula was easy: those with rooms on the ground floor would leave their sash windows unfastened, while nurses on the upper floors secured the services of an accomplice who, after the 'lights out' patrol, would unbar the fire-escape door, thus enabling the late-comer to steal indoors.

In such clandestine dealings status was forgotten. Yet while a junior could not expect any ward favours from senior colleagues for her services, these were deemed to be reciprocal, which convivially lengthened or widened off-duty activities, but also accounted for many a heavy-lidded nurse desperately trying to suppress yawns during her morning shift.

From the start I had been acutely aware of strong anti-German feelings among junior and senior staff, often expressed by no more than a tight smile on passing, or in addressing me solely on nursing matters. The 'Twins' had been equally quick in sensing an aura of hidden animosity which, at variance with our good will and friendliness, limited communication to the job in hand or requests for unbarring the fire-escape door. None of us, we agreed, had been guilty of making Teutonic waves or speaking German when in earshot of English colleagues. But then, we reckoned, the war had not been over long, and we first would have to prove ourselves.

One afternoon, helping herself to her third chocolate biscuit, a senior nurse neatly labelled two German second-year colleagues of ours.

'One is a slut, the other a bloody Nazi,' she said, not mincing her words, and the ready echo she found among her fellow nurses in the sitting room did not sound like a hasty defamation of character. On corner chairs, balancing a cup of tea on our knees, Lotte and I froze into the position of involuntary listeners who, by virtue of sharing the nationality of the subjects of disparagement, find their own reputation tainted. We stole glances at each other and, in a flash, I realized that our two compatriots had spoiled the atmosphere for us long before our arrival.

Nurse S. was overweight and in her late twenties. A full sensuous mouth and dark hungry eyes dominated a face curiously devoid of any light from within. Having a knack for repartees of the vulgar kind, and being flippant in her dealings with doctors and nurses, she was frequently reprimanded for turning up late or sleep-walking on duty. Now, with tongues sharpened, no secret was made of an earlier pregnancy which Nurse S. had carried to full term, before offering the baby for adoption and resuming her nursing career, nor of speculations likely to tingle every virtuous soul.

'I'll eat the new house surgeon's socks if she hasn't aborted at least once since.'

'Huuuh!' a cry went out, 'then it must be true.'

The incident proved that nurses commanding places at the sitting-room fire, and taking the pick of the tea-biscuits, were not particularly sensitive when it came to pillorying someone's morals or washing her dirty linen in public. But then, my own experiences soon gave credence to the vicious talk and rumours.

One morning I caught Nurse S. in the sluice, swallowing some pills.

'Amphetamine,' she said, 'something like a vitamin compound. It peps you up. I'm so darned tired.'

Her best smile. 'Do me a favour, Marianne, not a word to anyone, *ja?*'

Not much later, coming off night-duty, I watched her openly taking a handful of carmine-coloured pills.

'Iron tablets,' she explained. 'I always take them before my period is due . . . just to make sure it's coming.'

Small wonder, I thought, that her senior colleagues maliciously associated her off-duty activities with a horizontal position. In this they were finally proved right, when not long afterwards Nurse S. started to be sick in the ward toilet one morning, and five months later left the hospital with a well-rounded belly, never to be heard of again.

So much for iron tablets, I mused.

Nurse W. had perhaps done most in tarnishing the image of German nurses. Tall and thin, with a smile I had once seen on a child while it was crushing a beetle, her demeanour reflected something very linear and intransigent. It transpired that Nurse W. not only made no bones about her father's past as a high-ranking SS officer, but in a confrontation with staff she had justified his ideals and shrugged off the millions of gassed Jews as something 'regrettable', but 'tenable' in the nation's interest. Significantly, her shameful views and the overt flying of the Swastika banner in the democratic haven of an English hospital marked her not only as being incredibly brash, but downright stupid.

With such spoilers in our midst it was not easy for the 'Twins' and myself to break down the barriers of hostility. When we finally succeeded, we entered a climate of cold indifference. I alone had the dubious honour of rousing fierce sentiments of a different kind, of learning the hard way that where young women work and live en masse, surrounded only by young house officers and registrars, envy, jealousy and cattiness are never far away.

In my first year I developed a crush for the Resident Surgical Officer, something, nurses said, one caught and got over it, like measles or a cold. Yet while such an affliction was considered permissible, indeed unavoidable, it was nothing less than a sin for a student nurse actually to attract the attention of the adored surgeon.

Hero-worship had elevated Mr G. to a demi-god, capable of casting a sensuous spell on any female close to him. His languid smile, accentuated by an aquamarine flash of his eyes, never failed to bring colour to the palest of cheeks, and in his presence nurses were known to have dropped instruments or lost the power of speech, sisters to put on party faces.

Dark, and by virtue of his eyes which could send a receptive female's pulse into tachycardia, the Adonis of the operating theatre worked his strongest magic from the slit between his mask and cap, and junior nurses acting as 'runners', and likely to catch Mr G.'s attention, were warned to keep their eyes on the unconscious subject under his knife, when not counting swabs, fetching or carrying.

Out of mask and gown, Mr G. walked the wards and corridors in sartorial blue suits, his hands behind his back, his eyes fixed intently on the ground, as if in search of a lost object or listening to the ruminations of his mind.

It was my day off. Finding the nurses' home tennis court occupied, another junior and I ventured on to the senior staff's court, located close to, and in full view of the operating theatre.

Seeing patients watching from windows, I put all my power into dashing volleys and a strong serve. Someone applauded.

'Makes you feel like playing at Wimbledon,' said my partner.

I laughed and pushed my hair back. I felt good.

'My advantage,' I cried.

As I looked up to the theatre floor I thought I saw the ghost of a masked face behind the window.

'There she comes!' a voice from the theatre nurses' table greeted my entrance into the dining-room for lunch that day. And trumpeting my shame around, 'You should have seen G. this morning, looking over his shoulder through the window, every minute or so, in the middle of an appendicectomy . . . just to see Nurse Gaertner playing tennis. Looked like a love-sick dog, he did.'

'No wonder, what with the amount of thigh she was showing.'

'It's a miracle he didn't drop his scalpel.'

' . . . or a suture.'

Chuckles spiced with jealousy, contagious. The voice of the staff nurse, objective and professional:

'He's a liability in theatre when Nurse Gaertner is around!'

I found an empty seat, but the steak casserole proved too peppery for my taste, the treacle pudding too cloyingly sweet. However, hardened by Irish backbiting at the Radcliffe, I did not lower my eyes when I left the room, nor lose any sleep over the theatre staff's remarks.

Finally, at the Hospital Dance, I incurred even the Sisters' wrath, when Mr G. asked me to dance with him several times, and half-way through the evening disappeared with me into the wintry starlit night. It just was not done, set lips and arching brows intimated. After all, unwritten hospital rules decreed that junior nurses did not dance with senior doctors, let alone allow themselves to be lured by Mr G. from the dance-floor into heaven-knows what immoral activities. And I was sure it was no coincidence that next morning I was detailed to do the dirty-laundry count twice over for accuracy, and during visiting-time, to clean and tidy the ward's store-room, a cubicle stuffed with dusty crutches, drip-stands, leg cradles and various contraptions long superseded by more sophisticated nursing aids.

'Bloody jealousy!' commented Lotte, who was making good progress in the less refined areas of the English language.

In theory, all wards had to be covered by one junior and one senior while the rest of staff went for their meals. In practice, this rule did not always work, for wards never reached their full staffing complement due to holidays, sickness or off-duty rotas. Besides, there was a distinct advantage in opting for an early meal-break, when food came fresh from the hospital's ovens and cooking pots. Not infrequently, therefore, a probationer nurse might be left in charge of a ward at lunchtime when, fed and bed-panned, patients might enjoy a doze, and nothing untoward was expected to happen.

The responsibility of running a ward single-handed never over-awed me. On the contrary, my temporary position suffused me with a sense of self-importance, and I would walk around the ward an inch taller in the foretaste of seniority and wearing a staff nurse's green, silver-clasp belt or a Sister's blue uniform and frilled cap.

I was helping out on Maternity one day, when Sister and senior nurses went for their lunches.

'You should be all right, nurse,' said Sister, 'Mrs Mack is not due for delivery until later this evening.'

'But she says she's started contractions,' I insisted.

The Sister, a hospital gold medallist, who could get a job done before anyone else thought of it, and who moved up and down the ward as on roller skates, decided to indulge me, rather than put me in my place.

'So she has, but they are very weak. She isn't dilated enough yet, to start labour, not for several hours.'

Ten minutes later I knew that nature had played a trick on the normally accurate calculations of a sister and midwife, from whom, it was said, a young house officer could still learn a thing or two.

'Nurse!' shouted Mrs Mack, ripping the siesta calm of the ward apart. 'I feel the baby coming.'

I raced to her bedside. 'Are you sure?' I asked.

'Jesus, I ought to know, this is my fifth bairn,' Mrs Mack grunted, opening her knees and starting to bear down, while fiercely concentrating on her contractions.

'Try and hold it,' I implored the mother, furiously weighing up my chances of summoning help.

'I can't.'

What was I to do? The telephone in Sister's office seemed miles away, the dining-room was two storeys up. Around me, mothers sat up in bed, heads straining.

'Quick, nurse,' shouted Mrs Mack, 'it's coming!'

And now I rushed into action. I pulled a screen around the bed and inspected the hairy evidence of a foetal skull. Another tortuous moan, and the baby's head appeared, stretching the mother's perineum to the thinness of paper. With no time to don a mask or sterile gloves, I grabbed a towel from the delivery trolley. And now I knew what to do, what I had watched Sister do on a previous occasion.

'Take a deep breath,' I said, exuding a midwife's confidence, yet conscious of my racing pulse.

And seeing a new contraction rolling against the pain threshold,

'Push hard! That's it! Well done!'

Gently I eased the baby's shoulders free, then the tiny being slipped out between the knees of its mother who sank back on her pillows, exhausted, eyes wide open, waiting . . .

'It's a boy,' I said. 'Congratulations!'

But, oh, dear God, something seemed to be wrong. The baby's lungs were not opening in a lusty cry, none of its muscles twitched and its eyes remained closed.

The ward was dead quiet. For seconds, which dragged like the chained feet of convicts, I felt paralyzed. Then I remembered a film I had seen many years ago, in which the village midwife, upon delivering the farmer's wife, had held up the new baby and reluctant crier by its legs like a skinned rabbit, slapping it on its back, until the first cry pumped air into its lungs and filled the room with new life. It had worked in the film, I thought. It might work now.

And it did. The audience behind the screen applauded, Mrs Mack heaved a sigh, cried a little and said, 'Thank you, nurse.' However, instrumental as I had been in getting the baby to breathe, I had no idea, untrained as I was, whether obstetric rules barred me from severing the cord. I hesitated, a clamp in one hand, a pair of scissors in the other. Then, playing safe, I covered the baby up, left it snugly between its mother's legs and shot to the telephone.

Minutes later, Sister appeared, out of breath, a shadow of

self-reproach in her eyes. Quickly and skilfully she cut the cord, delivered the after-birth and helped me to make mother and child comfortable. Excitedly, the other patients did not withold their comments from her.

'You should have seen nurse! Not for a moment did she flap.'

'If it hadn't been for nurse acting so quickly . . . '

Sister's smile had long frozen.

'Will you come into my office, nurse,' she commanded.

She did not ask me to close the door behind me, which bespoke of minor censor not to be passed on to Matron.

'Nurse, you should have called me as soon as the patient went into labour. Anything could have happened.'

'But Sister . . . '

The Sister's stern look ordered me to hold my tongue.

'You may go for lunch now, nurse.'

On her day of discharge I saw Mrs Mack out, carrying 'my baby' in my arms. She introduced me to her husband, a sergeant with a ruddy complexion and a ready smile, and at his request I posed for a photograph.

'When is your next day off, nurse?'

'Next Sunday.'

'Well, if you have nothing better to do, would you like to come for lunch and for the afternoon? You could meet the rest of the family.'

'Yes, do come,' urged the sergeant. 'I have some photographs of Germany I'd like to show you . . . where I served with the Battalion. Do you like steak and kidney pie?'

Sunday lunch, however, proved to be what I took to be traditionally English – a roast joint complete with the proud trimmings of two vegetables, followed by baked apples and custard. Talk centred around barrack life, David's first molar, Angela's high marks in arithmetic and Cherry's recovery from a bad cold. Afterwards, seated around a gas fire in cover-worn chairs, the sergeant showed me photographs.

'Here's me and my two mates in a small village just across the German border. And, look, here's Herr Müller, the mayor, with his wife and children. And this is my platoon . . . '

No inquisition on Hitler, concentration camps or the war. No question either about my own background or my motives for coming to England. Instead, games with the children, who pay 'auntie' Marianne the compliment of letting her share their world. Close by, their father, mending a toy, lighting a pipe, humming a popular tune; buried in an armchair, the glow of the fire on her face, their mother, knitting children's socks. I am given the baby to hold. As it looks at me, the stranger, making little gurgling noises, his tiny hands tracing erratic patterns into the air, I feel something warm and wondrous erupt from where my maternal instincts are stored. Afternoon happiness complete with tea and chocolate cake. I have become part of a family.

For one Sunday afternoon.

A few weeks later, the wife of a titled patient, whose bare buttocks – due to the nature of his painful affliction – had become as familiar to me as the map of Berkshire, asked me over to their Datchet cottage for tea.

Overlooking a landscaped garden, French windows opened out to a groomed lawn over which a sprinkler was spreading a net of rainbow-coloured water particles. The sitting-room beckoned with cosiness, wooden beams and low ceilings, bowls of flowers, chintz, oak, pewter and brass. On the walls, miniature oil paintings flaunted beauty and value in oversized gilt frames. The tea-set was of silver, cups and plates of delicate bone china, the cucumber sandwiches were finely cut with just the right degree of moistness.

The hostess fitted admirably into such cultured surroundings. Her nails were pink and manicured, her pearls sat perfectly on a sleek dress of tailored simplicity, the kind one would look for in vain in Windsor's High Street shops. In harmony with her appearance her voice was soft, her accent royal, her smile consummate with the laws of hospitality.

In contrast, her husband who visibly enjoyed pile-free sitting comfort again, wore an open-neck shirt and lounged in his chair with the ease of a man who in his own home needs to make no concessions to a Sunday visitor, even less to a member of the lower nursing ranks. Nor did he deem English afternoon tea to be so sacrosanct as to forbid the questioning of a lady guest on subjects likely to detract her from the ritual or turn sour the agreeable taste in her mouth.

National Socialism, the SS, the Hitler Youth. The gassing of the Jews. The apparent lethargy of the German people vis-à-vis such policies. Familiar questions demanding an answer.

'And what did you think of Hitler?'

A piece of cherry cake gets stuck in my throat, makes me cough, grants me time. I am conscious of fragrance wafting in from the garden, of birds chirping away under the fine umbrella of spray, of the soft tinkling of silver, cups and cake forks – a background too delightful for questions of steel, no matter how delicately put, and forming too agreeable a climate to talk about cause and effect, crime and punishment, myths and truths, or about my father's own puppet role in the Führer's grand scheme.

The lady of the house tries to make amends.

'Here, Marianne, have another piece of cake. And perhaps you'd like to see the garden before you leave. The lilies are making a fine show this year.'

The time came when I had learnt the knack of giving painless injections with blunt needles and shaving pubic hair with a minimum of embarrassment; when changing dressings, removing stitches, dispensing medicines and monitoring post-operative patients had become routine duties, just as the 'laying-out' of the dead.

For me, this last sombre service had something of a celebration of the penultimate rites, as if by washing, the body was being cleansed of its emanations of suffering, fever, prurience or malignancy.

The confrontation with death and its inherent religious, moral and philosophical issues had a profound effect on me, and the very act of closing eyes, from which the light had gone, followed by the last ministrations on a pallid body, made me keenly aware of the thin line between this world and the hereafter. It also called my own good health and bubbling youth to mind. Sometimes, however, I faced the dying with a sense of utter helplessness, or with anger crying out, 'Why?', as in the case of a pretty seventeen year-old succumbing to peritonitis, whose life I watched running out, my eyes on an hour-glass.

Apart from cultivating punctuality, patience and tolerance towards the odious manifestations of some diseases, nursing was a great teacher of time-and-motion efficiency.

'Never walk up the length of a ward, nurse, without taking care of a patient, or bringing something back, on your way down!' Also, used as I had grown at the Warnford Hospital to mopping up spit and faeces, I found there was now no sight, no task so distasteful that I could not deal with it.

The long hours spent on night duty are etched in my memory. Not so much for fighting myself out of a leaden day-time sleep, nor for sitting down to warmed-up dinners at a time designed for sweet dreams and the ebb of body functions, but for the ambience of dimly-lit wards in which the stillness was brittle, likely to be broken at any time by a patient's snore, a moan, the clink of a glass or the call for a bottle or bedpan. And equally potent an image: nights made shrill and hectic by emergencies and the blinding light of the operating theatre, or remembered for the peculiarly stagnant odour of a ward, the whispered conversation with an insomniac, the echo of a death rattle, or for the hours when time appeared to stall and – to speak with Hamlet – even churchyards yawned and hell itself breathed contagion to the world. When, ultimately, reality narrowed to the glow of the desk lamp and Night Sister's round.

Nights on most wards usually ended by five am or earlier, when darkness still prevailed in winter, and a hazy light heralded dawn in summer. A last yawn, a mug of tea and a speedy morning routine would soon dispel the ghosts of the night. By the time the patients were washed and toiletted, urine samples had been collected, charts updated, fluids measured, the ward report written, and a cup of morning tea was settling the ward, the day staff arrived, morning glory on their cheeks and in their voices. Time to toddle off towards the cruel, loving daylight, in the hope that the long walk through the corridor back to my room, or a brisk sortie into town, would break the fetter of my ten-hour night shift, in which I stood on the periphery of my life, strangely divorced from the pulsating outside world of which I longed to be part.

Nursing was also a great educator, and even in the valley of routine jobs, there was always a lesson waiting. And how could anyone not find food for thought in witnessing the human spirit triumph over a body laid down with pain, injury or disease, nor marvel at how a patient's intense desire to return to a family fold, a job or the pleasant diversities of life would often hasten recovery like a miracle drug.

There were occasions when, for some clinical procedure, I had to wear a mask of indifference or asexual detachment, not to cause acute embarrassment, or reveal my own. It did not always work, certainly not when I went to catheterize a male patient in his late twenties, whose illness had not impaired his virility. Under the gentle touch of my hand and a cleansing swab, the patient's penis suddenly hoisted itself up like a flagpole, accompanied by the man's futile apologies. Trying to keep a blush in check, my hands returned to mid-air,. swab in one, a lubricated catheter in the other, while I studied the pattern of the screen's fabric, displaying maternal patience, until the emblem of masculinity had collapsed and was ready for urethral penetration.

By the time I passed my Preliminary State Examination I felt espoused to a career which, while steadily increasing my clinical skill, theoretical knowledge and the volume of human experiences, left little time for the development of my personality and tapered, rather than expanded, mental horizons. Few nurses, rarely if ever, read newspapers, and in the sitting-room senior nurses saw to it that the radio was tuned to *Mrs Dale's Diary* and the latest hit tunes. One day Lotte showed me a newspaper which she had retrieved from a patient.

'Did you know that there is a war on in Korea?' she asked.

I said I did not.

For me, everyday English was now coming quite easily, although occasionally I found myself not totally immune from the dangers of translating a German word into English all too literally, which often set a trap in *double-entendres*. One night such a slip evoked loud laughter which left me puzzled, rather than embarrassed.

I was attending a College dance, when some students crowded around me and asked me to list my German virtues and vices. Following a brief enumeration of my self-confessed strengths and weaknesses, I added 'And I'm also quite a fast girl,' thus alluding to my sprinting speeds during my years as an athlete. Surprised at the reaction which my innocent statement provoked, I pointed out, triumph in my voice, that my best time for the 100-metres had been 12.1 seconds, which instantly killed off the last salacious chuckle.

Lotte, forever stumbling over colloquialisms and ambiguous translations, was the cause of much English giggling one afternoon. Religious beliefs were under discussion in the sitting-room, a subject triggered off by the admission of a private patient of Moslem faith. Facetiously, a nurse suggested that he might want to use his bath-towel as a prayer-mat. And more out of boredom than academic interest she counted the number of Catholics and Anglicans present.

'And what are you?' she asked Lotte.

'I'm an Evangelist,' replied Lotte, being Protestant and, by virtue of literal translation, 'evangelisch'.

During my first few months at King Edward's life beyond the hospital confines or, at best, local city boundaries, remained remote. But once I had adapted to the disruptive routine of shift-duty, and learnt how to delicately balance my need for sleep with leisure activities that would revitalize the inner woman, widen my vistas or simply provide entertainment value, I began to settle down in what promised to become a career. On my days off I would take to the countryside on foot or by bus, or travel to London by Green Line coach, to explore the city tourist-style, eyes wide open and map in hand. I might go on a cruise up river, lose myself in the maze at Hampton Court, or satisfy my appetite for art at the Tate or National Gallery. I went to see screen classics, such as *La Ronde*, *Les Enfants du Paradis* and Disney's *Fantasia*. I met Philippe, a French student with a penchant for Baudelaire, and danced the Conga at the Foreign Students' Club. The hospital no longer dominated my life. And here was surely another lesson well learnt: if the world does not come to you, go out and seek it – even if, for me, at the end of my London outings, it meant sprinting like hell towards that last coach back to Windsor, and sending little prayers to heaven that I would find the fire-exit door unbarred.

In the spring of fifty-one my mother came over to spend a fortnight's holiday with me. She looked pale and tired, having made the twenty-eight hour journey from Berlin, first through the Russian Zone by bus, and hence to Ostend on the wooden seat of a West German pre-war train. I welcomed her at Victoria station with a single rose. We had not seen each other for over four years.

'How comfortable English trains are,' she said, her face regaining colour, the excitement of our Wiedersehen being amplified by milling concourse crowds and unfamiliar sights and sounds around.

As I steered her through the broiling London traffic, she appeared helpless, a first-time foreign traveller, a gentle middle-aged lady suddenly torn from the lone, hushed drawing-room atmosphere of her widowhood.

As the Green Line coach negotiated its way out of the city, she aired her first impressions.

'On the boat train, I could not help noticing the number of chimney stacks on English houses. A strange sight. So were the windows the train was passing – no lace curtains, unlike at home. You can stare right into the rooms. And what is it that people often stick right against a window? It's sort of oblong or rectangular, sometimes huge and obscuring the view?'

'A dressing table, *Mutti*. What you see is the mirror.'

I smiled. My own train journey from Harwich to London did not seem all that long ago.

Unlike myself, my mother had never been abroad before, and what she knew about English history and English people was patchy and remembered from school lessons: the Tower of London, the beheading of Mary, Queen of Scots, Henry VIII's dissipations, the country's 'brutal' empire building and the average Englishman's prediliction for tea, whisky and snobbery. And, not forgetting, life in London slums and Victorian child labour, gruesome subjects greedily exploited by the Nazi media.

1   The Radcliffe Infirmary, Oxford. 1948.

2   Radcliffe Infirmary, Oxford, the author's room under the fire escape.

3 Trudi, Lotti and the author at Preliminary Nursing School, Bay Court, 1950.

4 The author in the lecture room.

5 The author with her first-delivered baby
of Sergeant's wife.

6 King Edward VII Hospital, Mary Ward.
The author is the half-hidden
nurse on the right.

7   The Windsor Castle sentry as seen from the Nurses Home, 1952.

8   King Edward Nurses outside Westminster Hall waiting to pay their last respects to Queen Mary.
(By permission of the British Library.)

9   The author in front
of the Brandenburg Gate
1953, eight years before
The Wall went up.

10   The author, while
nursing at the British
Military Hospital,
Berlin-Spandau, 1954.

11 The author in Vicarage garden, Cookham Dean 1953.

12 Irene, the mongrel and author on Paguera beach 1955

13 The author and Irene at the well in the backyard of the Villa Miramar.

14 The author in the rock pool, La Calobra, Mallorca, 1955.

15   The author with her husband, 1957.

16   Their children, left to right, John 6, Donald 3 and Andrew 5, 1964

To this tableau of knowledge she could now add post-war images – Winston Churchill smoking an outsize cigar, and British Army uniforms and vehicles dominating the Charlottenburg area of Berlin.

I found my mother a room in a private household, and next morning she glowed with praise for the family who had welcomed her, unprejudiced and with much friendliness. They had also been most interested in what the first German they had ever set eyes upon had to tell about life in Germany under Hitler and during the war.

'Mind you,' my mother said, 'they had absolutely no idea of what conditions in the Russian Zone are like, and their knowledge about Berlin's special status was nebulous. I told them that the former capital now lies like an island in what we call 'The Russian Sea'; that at the end of the war it was divided into four sections and shared out among the victors like a cake. Then we had another 'nice cup of tea', strong, with milk and sugar.'

I laughed, for had I not myself become addicted to that 'nice cup of tea', the universal remedy, the pick-me-up and morale booster?

'And fancy,' my mother continued, 'this morning Mrs Pitcher did not only wake me with a cup of tea, but she also brought me breakfast in bed. What a luxury!'

I took my mother on a tour of Windsor Castle. Here, used to the stark visual sobriety of post-war Berlin and fascinated by the opulence of the staterooms, she stopped under every painting, peered closely at every gilded or gleaming object and every precious length of brocade. In St Georges Chapel, tuned in to its cathedral-like atmosphere and admiring the stonemasons' delicate craftsmanship, she merely stood hushed and clasped her hands. But when she caught sight of the many chimney stacks poking out of the roof of the royal residence, she aired her disapproval: 'What, even here? How ugly!' And walking through Eton High Street, 'Look, boys in tails. Why are they dressed up like that?'

We had 'afternoon tea' in tea-rooms opposite the Town Hall, where my mother asked for coffee, and after her first sip summed up her impressions of the brown liquid,

'It doesn't taste much like coffee.'

She also commented on the volume of traffic, used as she still was to a dearth of private motor vehicles on Berlin streets, and like the Oxford echo of my own sentiments, she found high praise for English queuing discipline and the politeness of the people we met.

Seeing children playing, dogs chasing each other and families unpacking their Sunday picnic boxes on the river's groomed grass verges or the smooth lawn carpets of Windsor Great Park, begged another comparison.

'Imagine, being actually allowed to sit and walk on the grass! Our public lawns are railed off, and signs forbid children to play and dogs to walk without a lead. Nobody would dare to step on them.' Or passing through a street lined with colourful gardens and trimmed front lawns: 'What a lovely sight! What a contrast to Berlin! There's still so much rubble lying about the city, and the weeds that infest ruins and what were once fine gardens often reach the height of a man.'

One afternoon, wanting to show off my mother, I took her into the nurses' sitting-room. All gracious smiles and 'How do you do?' she accepted an armchair vacated by a third-year nurse. I brought her a cup of tea and, to my surprise, was told to offer my mother some chocolate Digestives. As she sat, sipping her tea and nibbling a biscuit, the sun put highlights into her brown, wavy hair and enhanced the lustre of her single strand of pearls; it intensified the whiteness of her blouse and lent an air of *haute couture* to her wartime suit. Gradually, nurses resumed their conversation, but I noticed many a stolen glance at the beautiful lady in their midst, who had nothing in common with their pre-conceived image of straw-haired, slogan-shouting women of the Third Reich, and who looked more like a duchess.

During her stay with 'her family', my mother never ceased to be amazed at the various gestures of friendliness extended to her far in excess of traditional hospitality.

'You wouldn't believe it,' she said, 'they asked me to consider their house as my own. So much goodwill. I'm very moved.'

As I played tourist guide in Windsor and London, gently shoving my mother to the tail of queues and puzzling her with my liberal use of 'Please' and 'Thank you', if not with celebrating afternoon tea rites with the ease of one grown up with English middle-class customs, I mused how easily I had adopted some of the idiosyncracies of that way of life, and how far, how willingly, I had allowed my 'German-ness' to be eroded. I knew I was still a far cry from total integration – if this was at all possible with German roots, and if this was what I wanted. It might demand new loyalties, even the exorcism of memories. But how could I ever forget childhood prayers and childhood stories? How could I unshackle myself from a culture that had survived not only centuries, but the Nazi era, how, ultimately, from a period of my life when the fight for physical and spiritual survival had made me the person I was?

My mother and I went to Ilfracombe to spend a week by the sea. We walked through the green vales of the North Devon coastline and along paths close to high cliffs; we watched the sea in its changing moods, full of sheen and bonhomie one day, angry and broiling another, grey, dull and apparently motionless under a persistent drizzle. In town there was nothing that escaped my mother's comments. She marvelled at the number of people cleaning windows or busying themselves with brushes and white paint; she articulated her surprise at the amount of copper, brassware and tourist kitsch in shop windows. She looked intrigued at doors which had knobs instead of handles, and at wardrobes sized, she said, for the clothes of Lilliputians. She also commented on the number of women seen knitting, and of men walking or talking with their hands in their pockets – a habit which she neatly packaged as 'very English'. Anxious to conform to local customs, she learnt to say 'How do you do?', without expecting people to launch into their life histories or various ailments, and to restrain herself from offering German handshakes. She greatly enjoyed sausages, chips, custard and Devonshire cream teas, but asked why cooked vegetables tasted so bland.

For reasons of economy we stayed at Christopher St Epworth's, a guest-house recommended by my mother's Windsor hosts. Here, guests had a strong leaning towards religion, and towards Methodism in particular. Always quick to sing a hymn or say a prayer, they smiled readily and welcomed each new guest with brotherly and sisterly affection. A streak of asceticism was apparent in their attire, as well as in their modest demands on food and wordly holiday offerings. In line with their life-style, they neither drank nor smoked.

Needless to say, my mother and I joined such an unfamiliar holiday ambience with some trepidations. But any fear of possible attempts at conversion, or of our stay turning into one long Bible study, soon dissolved.

Despite my mother's statement that she was of Lutheran faith, and my own admission that I felt quite at home now in an Anglican church, our fellow guests – among them a few members of the Methodist clergy – did not put up sectarian barriers, but invited us to share their worship of a universal God in the evenings. This we did. Not so much so because it seemed customary at St Christopher's, but because its holiday-makers exuded an air of commitment, serenity and love for their fellow-beings, such as my mother and I had never before encountered.

And never before had I come upon English people whose questions about the war-time lives of ordinary Germans were prompted by Christian and Samaritan thought.

On the eve of our departure, the sitting-room community invited us to sing with them the German hymn, 'Now thank we all our God', which my mother remembered from her Sunday school days. Someone said a short prayer for us, before handshakes, good wishes and blessings sent us to bed.

Next morning, a painfully thin young man, whose clothes hung on him as on a scarecrow, presented my mother with a large box of chocolates.

'Here,' he said, as if handing his first date a bouquet of flowers, 'please accept this small gift . . . because you're a war-widow . . . because you've had such a hard time in Germany.'

'How very kind,' replied my mother, visibly moved, and helpless under the weight of compassion. But then she did not know any practising Christians in Berlin.

Wilhelm Furtwängler and the Berlin Symphony Orchestra were to give a concert in the Royal Albert Hall, their second in the capital after the war. Although, for some, he was still a politically ambiguous, for others a tragic figure, music lovers all over the world had long forgiven him for not having left Hitler's Germany. He had stayed on, he said, to keep music in Germany alive and free from Nazi infiltration. As a Berliner I knew much more: by musically uplifting thousands of hearts' with the strains of Beethoven, Brahms, or Mozart, he had not only fortified the spirit of music-devotees, but also sustained their trust in music as the sublime vehicle that transcends the obscenities of war. Indeed, Germans, and particularly Berliners, owed him much gratitude.

I decided to go to the concert, strong as my bond with Berlin still was, forcefully as my memory still retained some of the Homeric performances under Furtwängler's baton.

I queued for a cheap ticket, then raced up to the Gallery which commanded a fine view of the orchestra. Brahms, preceded by a Weber Overture, filled the first part of the programme, music stripping me of every care. An appreciative audience was generous with applause, before it settled down to the evening's highlight: Edwin Fischer, the famous German pianist, playing Beethoven's Fifth Piano Concerto, conducted by the maestro.

And now, as every chord, every harmonious cadence struck home, I grew tearful with that German 'inwardness' that tends to play on receptive nerves as on a Stradivarius.

A few minutes before the closing bars, I stole out of the Hall guided only by a vague idea of what to do next. My steps led me towards the artists' entrance, where police formed a cordon to a waiting car, and press and cameramen hovered about like hungry mosquitos.

I walked briskly, an expression of unconcern on my face, glancing neither left nor right. And perhaps because the absence of any hesitation in my gait and demeanour made me look like a member of the orchestra's retinue, police did not question me as I stepped through the side door, and the media's predators stared at me envious of apparent privilege.

Inside, in a corridor separating the soloists' room from the orchestral platform, I met Furtwängler and Edwin Fischer head-on. Behind them, tumultuous applause clamoured for their reappearance. Furtwängler smiled at me.

'*Na, was haben wir denn hier?*'[1] he asked.

---

[1] 'Well, what have we got here?'

'Herr Furtwängler,' I stammered, 'please forgive the intrusion. I only want to shake your hand. I was so moved. You see, I come from Berlin. I saw you conduct the *Pastorale* at the Berlin Philharmonic shortly before it was hit by a bomb. And I also saw you conduct *The Magic Flute* at the Admiralspalast.'

'*Ach, ja,* with Elizabeth Schwartskopf, an unforgettable performance. Everything was right that night, the orchestra, the voices, the mood . . . *Eine Sternstunde*[1]. One never knew in those days . . . ' His eyes glazed over, reaching back. 'And what an audience! *Ja, ja, das Berliner Musikpublikum . . . einmalig!*'[2]

'My grandmother was a great Beethoven lover,' I said, 'and one of your most ardent admirers, Herr Furtwängler. She never missed any of your concerts, and she often took me along.'

'My dear girl . . . ' Furtwängler began, only to be interrupted by a man in black tie, who pointed in the direction of the applause.

'If you please, *meine Herren*.'

Furtwängler shoved me gently into the artists' room.

'Wait here, *Kindchen*, don't go away. We have to take another bow.'

I was conscious of something very special happening in my life, in which for three years I had been working as an alien, remembering as a German, adapting myself to English customs, and flying high on English literary thought.

'Tell me,' asked Furtwängler, when the audience had finally let him go, 'what are you doing in England?'

I explained that I was a student nurse, and that I had first come over in forty-eight, to work, and to study English at Oxford.

'That couldn't have been easy for you,' said the maestro.

'It wasn't.'

'Have you got a programme?' asked Edwin Fischer, his pen at the ready. 'I'm sure you'd like us to autograph it.'

'I'm afraid I didn't have enough money to buy one. Student nurses . . . '

Furtwängler produced a programme, handed it to Edwin

---

1 a great evening
2 'Oh yes, Berlin concert and opera audiences . . . unique!'

Fischer, then signed his own name.

A few minutes later, richer, for two autographs, smiles and good wishes, I left the way I had come, unhindered, unquestioned, in my hand the treasured programme, on my face triumph, in my heart a warm feeling of music and nostalgia.

November 1952 was bitterly cold. Power stations raised their output, domestic chimneys furiously discharged smoke from coal fires. Unaffected by weather anomalies, industry continued to release its gases and smoke into the atmosphere. By the first week of December, when dense fog swirled in from the Thames valley, the air seemed to be appreciably heavier and to reek of the devil's kitchen. Obliterating the sun, the fog settled over Windsor like malignant breath; it crept through the streets and into alleyways, drifted into shops and cinemas, pressed threateningly against windows and finally seeped through crevices into rooms, where it put a yellow haze around lamplight. It muffled sound, and its particles of coal, oil and petrol irritated mucous membranes. In some people, it produced claustrophobia, in others a fear of choking, and among the old and sick it was to find thousands of easy victims in London and the Thames Valley alone.

The Great Smog lasted for three days.

On the first day visibility was down to a yard by afternoon. Traffic came to a standstill, cars were abandoned and pedestrians sensed their way home like the blind. By evening, visibility stopped at arm's length. Police and ambulances kerb-crawled to their destinations, their searchlights and sirens eerily deflected by the wall of fog.

I was on night duty on the Medical Ward of the Old Windsor Hospital, a few miles out of town, and a bus ride not normally exceeding ten minutes. As the night shift stood waiting to board the hospital bus, shivering, their cloaks pulled tightly around their thin cotton uniforms, the driver weighed up the chances of his vehicle reaching Old Windsor without ending up in the back of a parked car, against a tree, in a ditch or, worse, in a spongy river meadow.

'Jesus, what a pea-soup!' exclaimed a nurse. 'Has anyone got an oxygen mask handy?'

'It'd be like driving blindfold,' the driver told the Night Sister. 'I'm not suicidal.'

Sister, however, was determined.

'The day nurses need to be relieved, and patient care is always paramount,' she said, and authority finally won the argument. The porter fetched a torch and we climbed aboard. But when it took the driver ten minutes to negotiate the hospital gate and the road because he was unable to see beyond his dashboard, nurses jumped to the rescue. Pointing the torch as close to the kerb as possible, the first volunteer set out guiding the bus along.

Snail-paced, miraculously avoiding contact with solid objects the bus finally passed the city boundary, to creep along a country road visibly devoid of any form of life, and with mechanical sound restricted to the low-gear droning of the engine. And now that it was my turn to go on pilot duty, no kerb manifested itself under the beam of the torch and the ditch lurked no farther than a step or two. I walked wearily on the slippery road, torch trained on the asphalt, the bus uncomfortably close at my heels. Engulfed by thick vapour and obscurity, I soon felt displaced in time and space, an invader in some ghostly, hostile territory where sight was limited to the power of two batteries. And was it my imagination, or were they getting weaker by the minute?

An hour later, and with the last battery-operated glow, we arrived at the hutted ward accommodation which formed the hospital complex. Here, reality returned with a vengeance. Day staff stood waiting, tired, hungry, anxious and impatient. New batteries were found and the bus dispatched on its return journey. On my ward, fog had reduced visibility to the space between two beds, night-lights to glow-worms. The respiratory rate of patients with bronchial or heart trouble was rising dangerously. Worry on his face, a young house officer flitted from bed to bed, putting stethoscope to chests and oxygen masks into action. I brewed endless cups of strong tea, shook up pillows and walked the ward like a fog-shrouded Florence Nightingale carrying a torch instead of a candle.

The long night ended when daylight broke mockingly, suffused, impotent, victim to early darkness.

Two more mornings dawned similarly, then the fog lifted.

Newspapers calculated the number of deaths through bronchitis, pneumonia and heart failure in smog-affected areas at four thousand. Police rejoiced that the halcyon days for burglars and bag-snatchers were over. Doctors and nurses sighed with relief and fatigue. Chimneys, however, went on belching out smoke into urban skies – though fortunately not for much longer.

One morning, having completed a ten-night stretch on duty, I met Lotte on the way to our room.

'Christ, what a night!' she wailed. 'One appendicectomy, two admissions from Casualty and three fresh post-ops. And as if this wasn't enough, an elderly patient dropped his full urine bottle on the floor. You know, Marianne, they say it's summer.'

I fell in step with Lotte's mood.

'So they say. Ten nights on duty and you wouldn't notice if it snowed in June.'

'What was your night on "Gynae" like?'

'First half I was run off my feet with yesterday's hysterectomies. Then, between three and five, I would have given anything for a quick nap. But Night Sister kept popping in.'

Lotte stretched her arms. 'Ah, three days and three nights off. Have you got any plans?'

'Bed first,' I said, 'then a film, then bed again. As for tomorrow, I haven't decided yet.'

Lotte stared fixedly ahead, which always presaged an explosion of ideas.

'What if you and I were go to off somewhere, down south, hitch-hiking? Let's go to Portsmouth and watch the big ships.'

'Hitch-hike?'

'Yes, why not? We could come back by train. I feel adventurous and it won't harm us to leave the hospital miles behind.'

'All right,' I said, 'let's be adventurous. I feel I've been getting a bit into a rut myself lately.'

Neither of us gave any thought to whether we could make the south coast in one day and back, or where, with no more than a few pounds between us, we could spend the night. Just as if the coming off night duty, and the prospect of wallowing in sunshine, had made us footloose and fancy-free.

We stood waiting at the outskirts of Windsor like two innocents abroad, each raising a limp hand, in a gesture that would not have stopped a cyclist in his tracks. There was little traffic on the road over which the sun stood bright in a cloudless sky. From the river, the breath of morning meadows welled up. June beckoned, so did the freedom of the days ahead. How good it was to be alive.

Just then, a sleek limousine approached, its bonnet flashing in the sunlight. This time our hands went up more resolutely and the car stopped.

'Christ, isn't that a Bentley?' hissed Lotte, 'I hope the driver isn't a gangster.'

'Where are you going, ladies?' asked the man at the wheel, who looked exceedingly handsome, very aristocratic and not at all like a criminal.

'Portsmouth,' we cried.

'I'm going to Romsey, about half-way down south. Will that do?'

'Splendidly,' I replied. 'Thank you very much.'

The luxury of transportation, soft leather, low engine sounds aroused my senses. I gazed at the driver in the mirror, wondering how to strike up a conversation with this impeccably dressed gentleman of attractive middle age, whose features had something of sculptured Hellenic perfection. Just then his eyes momentarily strayed from the road, locked with mine in the mirror.

'Gosh, isn't he handsome!' I whispered to Lotte in German, totally forgetful of good manners. And, tongue-in-cheek, 'I wouldn't mind if he asked me for a date.'

With her feet always firmly on the ground, Lotte was not thinking of romance.

'He's definitely not a con-man,' she said between her lips. 'I guess he's a film star or some rich lord, or . . . '

The driver beamed an amused smile over his shoulder.

'What part of Germany do you come from, girls?' he asked in faultless German.

I felt myself shrinking to the size of a dwarf, while Lotte looked as if she had been caught in the nude. My voice was thin:

'My friend is from Freiburg, and I come from Berlin.'

'And what are you doing over here?'

'We are student nurses.' As eloquently as possible I stated

what had brought us to England.

'I have relatives in Hessen,' announced our chauffeur, not elaborating, not waiting for our reaction, and his charm now safely concentrated on the road. His running commentary on the Berkshire countryside, and observations on English weather, soon eased our initial embarrassment, loosened even Lotte's tongue.

'Excuse me, sir, are you perhaps in films?' she asked, her thick German accent strangely mitigating the boldness of the question.

The driving mirror revealed a broad grin, before Mr Handsome parted with the information that he was in the Navy, and on his way to Romsey Abbey to attend the christening of his niece. Whereupon he turned the conversation to post-war Germany, a subject which instantly settled us into adult behaviour.

As the car drew up in front of the Abbey, where a large crowd had gathered, an attendant jumped to open the driver's door. Cameras flashed.

'Did you see that?' said Lotte, itching to retrieve our former mood, 'I told you he must be someone famous or important. Let's get out.'

People stared at the two lanky young women who wore no hats, whose hair denied any recent subjugation to scissors, curlers or professional attention, and who were dressed as for a seaside promenade. A reporter, sensing a juicy addendum to his story, barred our way.

'Forgive me, ladies, but who might you be?'

Our Very Important Driver turned around.

'If you wait in the car, girls, I'll have someone drive you down to Portsmouth.'

A grin acknowledged the mélange of surprise and delight on our faces, and I tried to effuse our gratitude with a note of respect.

'Thank you very much, Sir.'

Back on the road, the uniformed chauffeur finally lifted the gentleman's identity.

'What,' he cried, 'you don't know who gave you a lift?'

Disbelief slackened his foot on the gas pedal.

'The son of Princess Victoria, who is the grand-daughter of

Queen Victoria. Until recently he was the Viceroy of India. Jesus, he's Lord Louis Mountbatten!'

Still dazzled from the earlier denouément, we stood ship-gazing at Portsmouth quayside, when three brown-skinned naval officers chatted us up.

'We're Pakistanis,' they said, 'allow us to introduce ourselves.' And a few minutes later, having established our nationality, and dismissed speculations as to our loitering intent, 'Would you like to see our ship?'

The tour, which took us to the bridge and deep into the bowels of the proud vessel, ended with an invitation to dinner in town.

'We always stay at a small hotel overnight, when we're on shore leave,' they explained. 'It would be an honour to have your company for dinner.'

Being impressed by the polite manners of our companions of an hour, and by now positively starving, Lotte and I allowed ourselves to be towed to a Victorian-style villa, where a Cerberian proprietor, antimacassars, gleaming brass and a large print of the Virgin Mary effused a God-fearing sobriety which dispelled any fears of entering a den of licentiousness. Besides, I reasoned, wasn't there safety in numbers?

Dinner, for which four more officers joined us, featured a variety of cooked and fresh vegetables, among them large bowls of spinach. Over a glass of cider we asked our hosts about Pakistan and India, a corner of the world which Lotte and I still associated with little more than the Taj Mahal and the river Ganges, curries, saris, heat, dust, beggars and holy cows, not forgetting the picture of an emaciated, saint-like man, called Mahatma Ghandi. In turn we answered questions about Germany, the war and Hitler. With a shock we finally realized that it was too late to make our way back to Windsor.

'Don't worry,' said the most senior officer. 'Allow us to fix you up with a room for the night.'

Lotte and I looked at each other.

'To hell with it,' Lotte breathed into my ear. 'Let's accept their offer. They're Muslims, I think. They haven't drunk any alcohol. Surely, they wouldn't dare ... would they? After all, we're nurses. Mind you, I hate to think what my father would say . . . '

'Or my mother.'

The proprietress handed us the room key as if it fitted the lock to her office safe.

'I've only got a single room left.'

She turned towards her bronze-coloured guests in the lounge, her eyes cutting to ribbons any possible speculations.

'You know the house rules, gentlemen!'

With German formality we bade our hosts 'good night' and went up to our room. Notwithstanding the high moral calibre of the hostelry, we locked the door behind us and, for good measure, secured it with a chair American Western style. We snorted with laughter when we eyed the prospect of sleeping in a bed made for thin people with short legs, but having robustly each claimed one half of the sagging mattress, and fought a tug-of-war with the blankets, we finally giggled ourselves to sleep.

'I'm afraid we won't be able to repay your hospitality,' I told the gentlemanly ambassadors of Pakistan over breakfast, while Lotte, busy with her cornflakes, mumbled something equally appropriate. As expected, our protestations of regret found a gracious echo:

'Please don't worry your pretty faces.'

'Just remember us in your prayers.'

'You were the first Germans we've met. We have to thank you for telling us about Germany.'

' . . . and for being such enjoyable company.'

Evening saw us safely back in Windsor.

'I can't wait until I tell my family that I rode with Lord Mountbatten in a Bentley,' said Lotte.

'And that we had ourselves picked up by Pakistanis like a pair of you-know-whats,' I countered.

Lotte looked over her shoulders.

'Pst, not a word to anyone. No one would believe that we slept like angels.'

*   *   *

A state of emergency was declared on the Male Surgical Wards, as the news of an accidental explosion at the nearby Combermere Barracks and home of the Household Cavalry reached the hospital. Nurses having a day off volunteered for duty on Casualty, shifts were re-arranged and George Ward made room for extra beds. Sister sent me to an early lunch.

'It's going to be a long day, nurse. Be quick about it.'

One by one the casualties were brought in, young soldiers suffering from burns or head and chest injuries. Sister dashed about, calm, astringent, soon bringing order into the chaos of the ward. I helped with the dressing of wounds, assisted in my first tracheotomy and kept the sterilizer on the boil.

Questioned by police at his bedside, the weapons instructor, a corporal suffering from facial wounds and the trauma of responsibility for his nineteen-strong squad of recruits, strongly denied any culpable negligence on his part. In no time his story leaked into wards and corridors.

Fully qualified in the use of grenades, detonators and gun cotton the handsome instructor in his late twenties had been familiarizing his squad with explosives, when in the heat of the summer sun and possibly due to an instability of the gun cotton, things had gone wrong during the demonstration. Now, playing down his own injuries, the corporal expressed great concern for his troopers, twelve of whom had been admitted to hospital, two in a critical condition.

'How are my chaps, doctor?' he asked, his head and part of his face in bandages.

'They're fine,' the house surgeon replied, not revealing that two troopers were fighting for their lives and one was not expected to last the night.

'What's your name, nurse?' the corporal asked me, when I had made him comfortable for the night.

'Gaertner.'

'I mean your Christian name.'

'Marianne.'

He took my hand. 'Do you mind if I call you Maria? You remind me of the woman Maria in the film *For Whom The Bell Tolls*.'

His eyes, in which the toughness of steel, a roguish twinkle and flashes of tenderness formed unlikely companions, perused my face. 'When I'm better, Maria, out of hospital, when this nasty business is over ... ' A tentative smile, restrained by muslin, and turning up only one corner of his mouth, finished the sentence.

But if his eyes had startled me, so now his mouth confused me with conflicting messages. For while the generous sweep of his lower lip suggested a disposition towards all things sensual, his upper lip was thin and set firm.

I could not make the man out. Yet something told me that the corporal was carrying more than a soldier's peace-time pack. What, I wondered, might there be asleep, buried or lurking behind the bandages and the soreness of the hour?

Next morning, the corporal learnt that Trooper Taylor had died. There would be an official inquiry, said the Commanding Officer, lowering his voice two decibels and fractionally his head. But the corporal was not to worry. First evidence suggested that he was not to blame. Besides, his fine military record would speak for him.

For the rest of the day, keeping his eyes closed or focussed on some distant scene, the corporal could not be drawn into the vaguest of smiles.

Towards evening, when the ward had quietened down, he called me to his bedside. His mouth and eyes softened.

'I feel lousy, Maria.'

'You're bound to,' I said. 'It's the shock. But then they say it wasn't your fault. So you should try and get some sleep.'

'I still feel responsible,' said the corporal. 'You see, it was different in the war. It was such a dirty war. And when you came back from leading an ambush, with some of your best chaps gone, you ground your teeth and cursed the Japs till you were blue in the face. You had no time to ask yourself whether a different strategy might have saved lives.'

'You fought in the war then?'

'Good Lord, yes. Burma mostly. Later I was recalled for Korea.'

'What, as a corporal?'

'Oh, no. I was a captain, acting major. I was a regular soldier, joined at seventeen.'

'Why then . . . ?' My question hung awkwardly over the bed.

'That's another story, Maria. It'll wait until you and I are alone.'

*　　*　　*

The time came when we were alone. When Michael was discharged from hospital with no more than a few visible scars; when Trooper Taylor had been buried with military honours and an official inquiry into the explosion had returned a verdict of 'Misadventure'. When, finally, the local press had exploited every angle of the affair.

Initially, we met after I came off duty in the evenings, and there would be just enough time to touch and forget, in the warmth of each other's arms, whatever, deep down, was troubling us, or had traumatized our souls in the past. And we did not waste words, nor squander precious moments on conventional overtures or trifling talk.

On my days off we walked in Windsor Great Park, holding hands and discussing life, books and poetry. Excitedly, we foraged through each other's minds and, like children, watched summer ageing week by week.

Many a balmy evening we would sit on some lawn, the first stars in the sky, our senses drugged by the waking scents of the night and the loneness of the hour – a setting all too tempting for a lovers' embrace. But my companion never lured me into a seductive position, nor allowed his self-control to wane. And whenever his voice acquired a deep, husky timbre and his breath quickened, I knew it would not be long before he would pull me back to my feet.

'Time, Maria, to go home.'

One day I asked him point-blank why, having reached the rank of acting major, he had ended up as a corporal and a weapons instructor.

'I resigned my commission after the war,' he replied. 'I wanted to get away from the feel of khaki, from the nastiness of war. From a war which I had survived, but which left me with a feeling that I had got off the train at the wrong destination – not where I wanted to be. If at that time you would have asked me where I thought I ought to be, I would have replied, "God knows".'

'I know the feeling,' I said, and told him about my own sense of disorientation after the war, and of the time when, following their divorce, my parents had deposited me in a Children's Home in order to get on with their own lives.

Michael pressed my hand.

'I realized, right from the beginning, that you were vulnerable, too, Maria. Perhaps it was one reason why I felt attracted to you.'

One day, in the Great Park, and under the auspices of an Indian summer, our relationship reached its turning-point. Tense, his eyes devoid of their ubiquitous twinkle, Michael pulled me towards him. From the beech tree above us, a soft breeze sent the first crinkled leaves floating to the ground. Symbolically, the last glow of daylight tinged the sky purple – the colour of truth, they say. There was peace in the air, an intimation of evensong and prayer, of a world temporarily stripped of its ills, and of darkness approaching on stockinged feet.

'I'm afraid it's "goodbye" for us, darling. We mustn't see each other again.'

'Why?' I cried.

'I'm not sure I can make you understand. You see, I am a tough soldier. I always thought of myself as hard and unassailable, given only to fleeting pleasures that asked for no gratitude or obligations, and made no demands on my conscience. Then you came along and cracked my outer shell with your own vulnerability and ideals. I began to see in you my better half, one that suddenly awoke to poetry and nature and – love. You provided me with a meaningful in-depth relationship, Maria, with the means for escapism.'

'But then . . . ' I stammered, bewildered, trying desperately to keep in step with Michael's train of thought.

He sighed. 'I'm sorry, but I'll have to spell it out to you in barrack-room language. You see, I'm afraid I can't keep my hands off you any longer. Yet I feel you deserve something better than a soldier's flighty love. And I'll be honest with you: in the past, my own instability made me reduce each new relationship to a one-night stand. Christ, I used to take a girl's pants off without preamble, without even asking for her name, just so that I could forget her immediately afterwards. But between you and me, Maria, there has been something almost sacrosanct.' He took a deep breath. 'I would destroy you, if I made love to you.'

Back in my room that night I was not at all sure whether I had fully understood Michael's reason for terminating our relationship. I tortured myself into sleep and next morning woke with an acute sense of loss.

A few days later, in lieu of a farewell note, and through the medium of a Shakespearian Sonnet, Michael tried to elucidate his decision.

'Farewell! thou are too dear for my possessing,
And like enough thou know'st thy estimate:
The charter of thy worth gives thee releasing;
My bonds in thee are all determinate.
For how do I hold thee but by thy granting?
And for that riches where is my deserving? . . .
The cause of this fair gift in me is wanting,
And so my patent back again is swerving.
Thyself thou gav'st, thy own worth then not knowing,
Or me, to whom thou gav'st it, else mistaking;
So thy great gift, upon misprision growing,
Comes home again, on better judgement making.
Thus have I had thee as a dream doth flatter;
In sleep, a king; but waking, no such matter.'

It was a difficult message for me to decipher, and although I read the lines over and over again, and pored over my dictionary, I did not unravel why someone could be too dear for someone else's possession. But then I remembered Daphne du Maurier's lines:

'If there was passion
I have forgotten it
If there was tenderness
It is with me still.'

And I knew I would never forget the tender, enigmatic corporal, just as I was sure no one would ever call me Maria again.

*   *   *

Castle Hill House, one of King Edward's Night Nurses Homes, stood directly opposite Windsor Castle's Henry VIII Gate, a perfect vantage point for the changing of the guard. It was, indeed, the prime view of the castle's precincts which one day caused me acute embarrassment. It also provoked some heat-affected nurses into staging a titillating show which incurred Matron's grave displeasure.

King George VI had died and Windsor got ready to pay the King its last respects. Lotte and I, coming off night-duty, were among those issued with a Pass admitting the bearer to Windsor Park, to watch the funeral procession from the Long Walk.

Although the day had broken bitterly cold, a clear February sky spread none of the miasmic sadness that so often forms the background to a funeral. With my cloak pulled tightly around me, and shivering as much from the frost creeping under my cotton uniform, as from the sight of bleak faces around me, I experienced an emotional moment when the draped coffin slowly passed me on its gun carriage. Not because a king had died, about whom I knew next to nothing, and who in his lifetime had not affected my own sphere or patriotism, but because many women in their homage made the sign of the cross or gave a half-curtsey, men bared and bowed their heads and an old woman wiped away a tear. People along the route represented a whole nation mourning the passing of their monarch – something to which there had been no parallel in Germany in my time. Conscious of a pang of envy, I compared their tribute to a dead king with the reaction the news of Hitler's death had prompted in my fellow-citizens in 1945. Then, the unashamed, the fearless heaving of a sigh had expressed relief, eyes had remained dry and voices grown steadily brighter. 'Let's get on with what he's left us!' had been the slogan of the new era. In the vale of their fatigue, hunger and sorrow, they had not mourned the Führer's death, but the brutality and futility of a war that had taken so long to end.

Back at Castle Hill House, a twelve-deep crowd had gathered on the hill and along the Castle to the Round Tower, and still more people were arriving, some carrying bunches of daffodils or spring posies, to lay down on the lawn besides the countless wreaths. Outside the Gate, a long line of carriages and gleaming limousines stood waiting, to take back to London the Royal family, Ministers of the Crown and Church dignitaries, as well as four foreign kings, five queens and several Heads of State attending the funeral ceremony at St George's Chapel. Despite the cold every front window of Castle Hill House was wide open, with night nurses enjoying a view as from the Royal box of Windsor's Repertory Theatre. While Lotte had found herself a space at an upper window, I had secured my own at ground floor level, where all the pushing and jostling suggested that a close-up of so many crowned heads and statesmen might be the chance of a lifetime. As we waited for their departure, comments, relieving tedium or tension, yet unlikely to offend the solemnity of the hour, passed between the onlookers on the different floors. At the bottom of the hill the crowd stood waiting, still, stoically, in silence.

When the proud carriages and limousines finally drew up, excited voices in Castle Hill House windows identified the illustrious mourners like children do their favourite cartoon characters. And now, instantly spotted for his conspicuous features, a darkly-clad Konrad Adenauer took up a waiting position right under my window, at his elbow President Auriol of France.

Leaning far out, my head turned upwards to where Lotte was watching the spectacle, and involuntarily slipping into German, I cried out,

'Look, Lotte, there's our President!'

Adenauer turned, looked at me and shook his head.

'Chancellor,' he corrected, and again, smiling with an old man's indulgence, *'Kanzler, meine Dame.'*

My face held an apology. But how could I explain that I had been too wrapped up in hospital life and escapist dreams, to keep abreast with political developments in Germany.

Adenauer's curiosity took over.

'You are German?' he asked.

'Yes, I'm from Berlin.'

'And I'm from Freiburg,' roared Lotte from her window.

Adenauer's smile split to his ears.

'Hm, what are you doing over here?'

'We're student nurses,' I replied. 'There are four of us.'

Just then a chauffeur invited the Chancellor and President Auriol to climb into a limousine.

'Well then,' Adenauer added in his broadest *Kölsch*[1], raising a

---

1 Cologne dialect

didactic finger, 'make sure you girls learn as much as you can. We need good nurses back home. *Auf Wiedersehen!'*

Windsor lay simmering in a July heatwave, when I returned to Castle Hill House. I was annoyed that only two months after finishing twelve weeks of night duty I was back 'on nights'. But then I knew why the sudden change of rota smacked of a punishment posting. Matron, forever trying to find fault with me, had at last managed to get her teeth into me, by catching me smoking a cigarette in the hospital corridor as I came off duty.

It had been a long day: several operations, one emergency and a minor crisis on the ward. I was tired, my armpits were damp, my legs felt as if they had run a marathon. A smell of Jeye's fluid and rubber 'mac' was clinging to my hands like gloves. A few puffs would bring down the shutters behind me, I thought. Then a bath, a book, sleep. It was the moment Matron materialized from apparently nowhere, surprise patrols being her forte. My hand with the cigarette went behind my back. But long before she was level with me, Matron sniffed the air like a tracker hound.

'Are you smoking, nurse?'

Slowly, my burning cigarette produced the evidence.

'Report to my office first thing in the morning,' she said in a voice that left no room for an apology.

At Castle Hill House, shortly before noon, High Street traffic noise was pounding through the open windows into bedrooms that resembled hot-houses. Small wonder then that many nurses were still up, some of them lounging about in the sitting-room, barefooted, their dresses unbuttoned. Cursing the heat, night duty in general and their swollen feet in particular, they longed for a swim, for the coolness of a breeze or for anything that would either pep them up or send them to sleep.

At the Castle Gate opposite, framed by the open window, a sentry was keeping a lone watch, untroubled at this broiling hour by casual visitors, tormented only – so nurses speculated – by the heat under his bearskin.

'I wonder how much he can take?' said a nurse and, positioning herself close to the window, began to take off her dress in full view of the soldier, slowly, teasingly.

Suddenly, the atmosphere in the room was charged with encouragement.

'That's it, well done! Anyone would think you're a professional strip-teaser.'

'Now the bra. Take your time. One by one.'

'Let him stew!'

The sentry, his sight trained on one bare breast, the angle and size of which might well be found in many barrack-room locker, did not stir. But neither did his knees buckle under him.

'Christ, he must be blind.'

'Come on, give him the bloody lot!'

The stripper inched another breast out of its constriction, then stood naked from just below the navel, her pants rolled down to the wings of her pelvis.

'He must be frying now.'

'I say, isn't he swaying a bit? Try a belly-dance.'

Just then a car drove through the gate, stopped abruptly, and hastily reversed back into the castle forecourt. The sentry, snapping out of what he might have taken for heat-induced hallucinations performed a few 'one-two-three forward, turn, one-two-three backward, steps.

The spell was broken. The game was over. The strip-teaser retreated to the bathroom for a shower and a junior nurse offered to make tea and toast.

Not more than twenty minutes later Matron, sternly assisted by Home Sister, stormed into Castle Hill House.

'Who is responsible for the most disgusting exhibition that took place at this window not long ago?' she demanded, summoning every nurse, whether in bed or not, to the scene of the crime. Her eyes flashed, the colour of her cheeks was high, her bloodless lips had thinned to a slit.

'How do I know?' she screeched. 'The Commanding Officer rang me. He saw one of you at the open window, stark naked, in full view of the sentry. I want to know which one of you disgraced herself in such a shocking manner and gave King Edward's nurses a bad name.'

By now the atmosphere in the room was as oppressive as the heat outside. Silence prevailed.

'Well then, as from now, you will all be under house arrest between shifts, until the person responsible for this disgraceful spectacle has the decency to report to me.'

Suddenly, Matron hurled a look at me like a flaming torch, as if only an alien could have been the instigator of such a show of impropriety, or worse, have enacted it. In the climate of the room my mien of innocence crumpled under the guilt of passive participation.

Back in my basement room, lying naked between sheets, I felt suddenly very tired, very unsure of my maturity and of being in the right job. As the room with its barred windows invoked claustrophobia, I saw the outside world hidden behind a wall of mist. Images assailed me, of sinking deeper and deeper into the quagmire of routine, of being no more than a useful pair of arms and legs, watched over by super-efficient sisters and a Matron from whose eyes, within seconds, the fury of a volcano could erupt from an iceberg. Yearning for a beach, for the cool shade of Black Forest pines, for the dream-like quality and velvety waters of 'my lake' in Potsdam, on which I had once reigned like a queen for the eternity of summer, I fell asleep.

By the time I went on duty that night our house arrest had been lifted. Back at Castle Hill House the following morning, I saw suitcases waiting by the door, their labels bearing the stripteaser's name.

At Henry VIII Gate, a lone bearskin sentry stood his watch, his eyes, drill-like, focussed on the empty windows opposite.

He might have been a wax figure from Madame Tussaud's.

*   *   *

Queen Mary had died and was lying-in-state in Westminster Hall. Matron decided that a complement of third-year nurses were to go to London, to pay their last respects to the Queen on behalf of King Edward's staff.

The day was marked by truly funereal weather. Low temperatures and a heavily overcast sky promised sleet or rain. Indeed, by the time our coach arrived in Parliament Square, it was drizzling. A mile-long queue, in which people stood silently, three abreast, wound its way from the Hall past the House of Parliament down to the embankment. Umbrellas were sticking out of the vast human triangle like mushrooms, and the solemn faces of the people waiting to file past the Queen's coffin, spoke of their determination to spite the cold and the rain.

Police were giving priority to nurses, and we soon found ourselves positioned not far from the entrance. The waiting and the slow forward crawl began. Suddenly, a gust of wind blew under my cloak and cotton frock, brushing my thighs and settling on my lower back like a wet towel. I shivered, and I was wondering whether any of us, young as we were, and normally not bothered by a cold draught up our skirts, had started out that morning wearing a pair of warm panties. As if she had read my thoughts, a nurse behind me articulated such speculations.

'Christ, I wish I were wearing my bloomers!'

Amused at this blunt statement which, delivered in a deadpan voice, momentarily relieved the monotony of waiting and, for me, as a collector of English witticisms, instantly brought to mind the more provocative simile of 'passion-killers', I turned my head and flashed a cognisant smile over my shoulder.

It was the very moment a nearby press photographer clicked his camera, the moment also when the Great Shunter of human lives stepped in and decided upon my future in nursing.

In the dim light of the ancient Hall, the monumental peacefulness of death manifested itself in the soft, reverent shuffling of hundreds of feet. So this is the famous Hall, I thought, where Charles I was tried and sentenced to death, Oliver Cromwell's head hung from a gable and former kings and queens had lain-in-state. Where now, amid the munificence of mourning, a tableau worthy of a dead queen evoked a sense of history and tradition: a coffin draped with the royal standard and white flowers. The presenters of pageantry: guards in scarlet tunics and white plumes, with swords and pikes. And once again, as during the late king's funeral procession, ordinary people adding a personal note to their homage – poignancy transcending the formidable public body of mourning.

In tune with the sombre event and the weeping sky we rode back to Windsor in silence.

Next morning, at the stroke of ten, I was summoned to Matron's office. Seated rigidly at her desk, her eyes breathing fire, she seemed to spit out each word from a reservoir of anger deep within.

'Nurse,' she said, holding up an evening paper and pointing to a photograph on the third page, 'have you seen this?'

I moved closer and saw myself standing in the queue of mourners outside Westminster Hall, framed by solemn-looking nurses from King Edward's. I was facing the camera, smiling.

'You have disgraced the hospital,' Matron said, in a voice capable of cutting through metal. 'If it weren't for your Finals in two months' time I'd send you back to Germany tomorrow.'

With a final sweep of her hand and an expression of utter disgust she dismissed me.

Within hours, the institutional jungle drum had carried the news of my disgrace to every member of the nursing staff. As a result, and perhaps for the purpose of atonement, the ward sister told me to give the sluice a 'jolly good' clean-up – a job normally delegated to a junior or an auxiliary. In the dining-room during lunch I wished I were invisible, and I gave up my roly-poly dessert for a quick escape. In the nurses' sitting-room that afternoon, I was finally 'sent to Coventry', where I stayed until, two days later, I predictably found myself back on night duty on the busiest ward of the hospital.

Things really came to a head when a nurse had her purse stolen from her room and someone alleged having seen me entering it. I was reported to the Domestic Supervisor, interrogated by the Home Sister and confronted with those who, for fear of finding the culprit among their own kind, pick an outsider, preferably a foreigner, as an easy suspect and pronounce the person guilty in a case unproven. And no matter how strongly I protested my innocence, and although a search of my room failed to produce the *corpus delicti*, convenience labelled me a thief, an accusation which I would bear on my shoulders like a ten-ton weight till the day I left the hospital.

'Nobody believes me,' I told the Hospital Chaplain whose wife I had nursed for two weeks before she died of cancer. The gentle, softspoken Canon, whose black hair, black eyes and black robe made him look more like a Prince of Darkness than a man of the cloth, listened sympathetically, before he dispensed consolation.

'My dear girl, if you're innocent, the guilty person will be found. Perhaps not today, perhaps not tomorrow, but one day. Justice is often slow in clearing a name.'

'I feel I've become a universal scapegoat,' I sobbed.

'When are you leaving the hospital?' the Canon asked.

'Straight after my Finals, at the beginning of June.'

'And where will you be going from here?'

'I'm not sure yet. My work permit expires in November. I've applied for a midwifery course at Kings College Hospital in London, and I've been for an interview. They explained that once an applicant has passed her Finals, it was customary to seek a reference from her training school. Now, after what I told you, can you imagine our Matron giving me a glowing testimony?'

The canon scratched his blue chin.

'Why don't you come and live with us at Cookham-Dean for the summer? Now that my dear wife is dead, the vicarage seems rather large for my daughter and myself. We have a local woman who comes in to clean. You could have a good rest first. Then, if you like, you could help my daughter with dinner and go shopping in the village when she's at work. We have a horse, a dog and two cats, and there's a good-sized vegetable garden. Please say you'll come. You'd be good company for my daughter and me. Cookham-Dean is a lovely, peaceful village. It lies on a hill. And you should see the cherry orchards! Someone even wrote a poem about them . . . '

Before the Canon had ended his description, he had already sold me the place.

'Thank you very much,' I said, 'I'd love to come.'

The Finals. With the various written papers and the first part of the GNC Practical Exam over, I faced the Ward Exam with confidence.

The Sister questioned me on medicines and solutions, and critically eyed the trolley I had prepared for a lumbar puncture. Unable to fault me, she then set what she must have hoped was a sure trap.

'Go and pass a stomach tube on Mrs B., and set up a milk drip for a gastric feed.'

Not that such a task was beyond a Third-Year nurse's capabilities, nor a request for its demonstration unfair in a Final exam. It was the name of the patient on whom I was to prove

my skill, which mobilized my adrenaline. For the gullet of Mrs
B., a middle-aged lady, had not only driven staff nurse and
sister, but also the house surgeon to distraction that morning,
by resisting every effort at passing down a thick length of
tubing. Here, at last, by virtue of the candidate's likely failure,
an opportunity presented itself for Matron to settle her final
account with me.

During the demonstration, the Home Sister, deputizing for
Matron, the Ward Sister and an official GNC examiner stood at
the foot of the patient's bed like stone pillars, their faces blank,
their eyes ready to spot any wrong procedural sequence, any
careless movement likely to upset the patient or endanger the
success of the operation.

This is it, I thought, feeling an oil slick under my feet and my
hands warning me of their uncoordinated action. What chance
did I have, where more experienced intubators had failed? But
now my spirit of defiance, which in the past had often stood me
in good stead, infused professionalism, spread confidence in my
veins. My lips tightened. Let's show them, they said. And I
remembered the time I had been in hospital with jaundice and
hepatitis, and a doctor had passed a tube down my throat.
How, having instructed me to hold my breath while swallowing
as hard as I could, he had accompanied the procedure, singing
'Schluck, schluck, Mä-ädchen, schluck'[1] to the operatic tune of
'Trink, trink, Brüderlein trink . . . '[2]. How afterwards, he had
patted the seventeen year-old on her back, 'Well done!'

With such successful technique in mind I now set upon my
difficult task, not rushing the job, so as to avoid too much
friction triggering off the gullet's reflexes. And it worked.
Smoothly, I connected the tubing and adjusted the milk drip.
The patient smiled. Radiant inside, I displayed the composure
of one who had done no more than a routine job.

'I hope you like milk, Mrs B.,' I joked, before facing my
judges.

'Thank you, nurse,' said the examiner, not flexing a muscle,
not betraying with the flicker of an eye lid that I had passed. The
Ward Sister attempted a thin smile, while the Home Sister hid

1 'Swallow, swallow, little girl, swallow . . . '
2 'Drink, drink, brother, drink . . . ' (from the *Student Prince*)

herself behind her ever-stern mask.

Next day I left King Edward's. With no regrets, but with a feeling that in three years I had amassed knowledge and skills that might prove invaluable allies wherever life would lead me. And though the shadow of a false accusation and of that damning photograph were hanging over my departure, I walked out of the hospital, my head held high in a final protestation of innocence and defiance. I did not look back. There was no need to. I had finished my training in the face of many odds. It was all that counted. And, not to have given up when the going had become rough or the draught from enemy quarters too cold. But then it was not the first time that perseverance – King Frederic II's Prussian-style dictum – had delivered its own sweet rewards.

With rose-coloured thoughts and spring in my gait I walked into the open arms of a young summer.

6

In the footsteps of Messrs Mole and Badger

'He cannot know who has not seen
The cherry orchards at Cookham Dean,
Who has not seen the blossom lie
Like snowdrifts 'gainst a cloudless sky
And found the beauty of the way
Through lanes bedecked with petalled may.'
Gone Rambling (Cecil Roberts)

Once again I was acutely aware of the change of scene: I had left behind the smell of disinfectant and floor polish, the daytime hustle and bustle of wards, the eerie night-zone of apparent timelessness, the rigid attention to rules and routine, the harnessing to a hierarchical order and, often enough, jobs odious or repulsive in nature. Reality, as well as an aching back and tired feet, had taken the glamour out of nursing. But in its place there had been born a sense of humility and caring, while experience had cultivated a capacity for applying acquired skills and common sense to any given situation – returns not measurable in pounds, grading or handshakes.

Now, spaced only by a half-hour bus ride and, for the last mile, by a twisting road lined by tiers of beech trees and meadows heavily fringed by willow herb, I found myself in the picturesque village of Cookham Dean.

Century-old trees, private residences hiding behind flowering shrubs or dense hedges, wood-and-brick cottages. A generous village green. Verdant space roofed by a blue sky and dotted white, yellow and pink.

Seemingly untouched by time, the village commanded a hilly site and was surrounded by cherry orchards, the late bloom of which shone 'gainst the cloudless sky like snowdrifts'. I soaked up the sweet scents of early June blossoms. My eyes, used as they had been to clinical whiteness, and the pallid or sunken look of illness, danced merrily over the pleasing vistas around me. At the thought of spending an entire summer on this Arcadian spot, the last three years fell away from me as an empty cocoon.

The Vicarage, which begged comparison with a Manor House, stood in a garden dominated by majestic beech and Ilex trees, its back lawn inviting images of croquet games, tennis and tea-parties. At its far end, delineated against the misty darkness of a distant forest track, the crowns of cherry trees peeked over a box hedge. On its western side, bordering on the cemetery and the grounds of the mid-nineteenth-century village church, overhanging branches formed a natural arboreal arch to a bay window, under which sunlight and shade created fitful patterns on the grass. Separated by flowering shrubs, a vegetable garden displaying rows of emerging lettuces, carrots, brassicas and herbs promised fresh fare straight on the table. At the northern side of the house, in the shade of a miniature copse, a horse stood nibbling some leafy delicacy.

The perfume of mature lilac and cherry blossoms wooed my senses. There was peace in this pastoral symphony to which birdsong and the capricious rustling of leaves added discreet incidental music. A Berkshire Garden of Eden, I thought, a place spinning a fine web of magic around me, as my lake in Potsdam had enchanted the young romantic, or Lake Como from the Villa Carlotta on a simmering summer afternoon. As other sights and sounds had done, often for no more than the privilege of minutes.

Canon Moore, who had moved to Cookham Dean shortly after his wife's death, now lived with the second eldest of his six daughters. Patricia, a post-graduate Biochemistry student at London university, was away for the best part of the day. Not surprisingly, the monastic silence and emptiness of the ten-room Vicarage had created a sense of loneliness for the widower, with which – despite his rounds of parochial duties – he had not yet come to terms. And he freely admitted that his innermost communion with God whom he was serving so devotedly had so far provided insufficient solace, used as he had been to his last appointment as hospital chaplain and, apart from his years at Cambridge University, to the colourful buoyant life in his parish of St Michael, on Barbados, the island where he was born and had lived for most of his life.

I was delighted with my room, which was large and bright and faced a cloud of pinkish blossoms mere feet from the window. I was no less affected by Patricia's friendliness and her own admission that she welcomed in me not only a companion for her father, but also someone who would hopefully lift some of the housekeeper's burden off her shoulders. Indeed, coming home after a day's work and a testy hour of commuting, she appreciated that she could now sit down at a ready-laid table, and to dishes which, whilst not denying their German origin, enticed father and daughter to second helpings. At the cooker I gratefully remembered the cooking lessons my grandmother had given the teenager: cordon-bleu demonstrations ranging from the secret of how to create potato puree perfect in consistency and taste, to the initiation into the art of preparing a sauce béchamel.

I soon mapped out my daily routine.

In the mornings, I would walk to the village shop, a basket over my arm, sunshine on my face and Tinker, the terrier, never far from my heels. Initially, curiosity greeted me from either side of the counter, leading to tentative conversation. I might be a foreigner, even a pretty German, the villagers' unsure smiles or their well-weighed sentences intimated, but their Vicar had invited me for the summer, and his daughter had befriended me, so I was bound to be a person of some merit. And it was not long, before we discussed the weather or the price of bacon, and I parted with my grandmother's recipe for Berliner apple cake.

Later in the month, I picked the first herbs and lettuces, and checked the carrots for their dinner potential; I cut fresh flowers and sat at the kitchen table, chatting with Daisy, the char-woman, over an 'elevenses cuppa'; I cooked soup for lunch, played with the dog, stroked the cat and tried to communicate with the mare. Sometimes I got busy with needle, buttons and thread. And there was always time for a stroll with the Canon through quiet country lanes, during which my companion gently questioned me about my parents, life under a dictator-ship, and about a war from which he and his family had been distanced on their Carribean island as on another planet. Affected by my frank narrative, he probed into the cause and effect of Hitler's rise to power, and when I told him about the agony and impotence of the German people, who had paid dearly for their gullibility, their blinkered vision and their 'Heil Hitler' choruses, he listened like a child to fairy tales. One day, when I spoke about the years which I had branded the 'naked' ones, he slipped his arm through mine. 'My dear child . . . '

But sympathy for my own battle wounds was the last thing I wanted. I knew the arguments by heart: had I not survived? Weren't others much worse off, and wasn't all former German suffering overshadowed, put in its place, as it were, by what after the war had been termed the 'Holocaust'?

Brushing off the Canon's proffer of sympathy, I said:

'Please tell me something about your life on Barbados.'

In the afternoons, the two of us would have tea at the open bay windows of the lounge – finely-cut cucumber sandwiches, cake or biscuits baked to my grandmother's recipes, afternoons not made for the quicksands of memory, but for the sunlight filtering through the trees, streaking and chequering our faces; for conversation bubbling through mundane meadows or examining the cataracts of life, and at least once a week, for my being allowed to select a theme for the Canon's Sunday sermon.

My involvement in vicarial affairs had started on one such afternoon.

'What do you think I should preach about next Sunday, Marianne?'

'Why, have you run out of Bible passages?'

'No, of course not. I just thought you might suggest one close to your heart.'

'I'm afraid the last time I held a Bible in my hand was at my Confirmation.'

The Canon was not to be put off.

'I'm sure one will have stuck in your mind. I mean, the way you seem to have coped with your life . . . '

'At Sunday School we had to learn "The Lord is my shepherd" by heart, and my Confirmation text was a passage from the *I Corinthians*, which ends, "But now abideth Faith, Hope, Love, these three . . . ". But there is one line which acquired a special meaning for me, because it often served me well. Whether during the bombing in Berlin, when you counted the seconds before the next impact, on the refugee trek, when the cold posed a greater threat than the Soviet troops at your heels, or when I tried secretly to cross the border into the Russian Zone and was taken prisoner by Mongolian soldiers.'

The Canon's face registered the thousand of miles that had separated Barbados from war-torn Germany. His voice was hoarse.

'And which line was that?'

'Fear thou not, for I am with thee.'

Now the Canon was back on his own territory.

'Ah, what a glorious passage . . . so fortifying. Isaiah forty-one, verse ten. May I have another cup of tea, Marianne?'

That evening I found a present in my room: a fifty year-old Bible inscribed, 'For Marianne who feareth not'.

The following Sunday morning, and every Sunday to come, I attended Matins, my roast safely deposited in the oven, potatoes peeled and two vegetables ready for cooking. I sat in the front pew, wearing a hat in English church-going fashion and listening to a sermon for which I had supplied the theme or the leading passage.

And I knew it was good to be living in Cookham Dean.

Early in August two of the Canon's daughters came to stay for a few days. To introduce them to his parishioners, and to make up for the absence of a traditional English church fête that year, the Canon arranged for an open-house garden party.

I baked and prepared mountains of sandwiches; I wore a dress that did not give me away as a foreigner and, as if village born and bred, I joined the conversation on the lawn, smiling, replenishing tea cups and not forgetting to pass comments on the weather. I felt marvellously 'English' and, for one whole afternoon, as if I belonged.

'Did you know that this area is famous for two delightful books?' asked the Canon. At Cookham, Jermome K. Jerome wrote his *Three Men in a Boat*, while Kenneth Graham, the author of *The Wind in the Willows*, lived in Cookham Dean as a child. They say that it was down at the Cookham stretch where he was introduced to the magic of the Thames.'

'I vaguely remember reading *Three Men in a Boat* in German at school,' I said, 'and after the war struggling through *The*

Wind in the Willows – a present from an English soldier.'

'Then you must read the books again, so that you can see the river and the woods through the eyes of the main characters.'

The Canon went out and returned with two books.

'Here, they belong to my youngest daughter, she read them on Barbados as a child. As she had never been to England, she was absolutely fascinated with the author's evocation of the local landscape.'

I read the books. And now nothing could hold me back from searching for the tracks of those lovely protagonists. Like a child I would set out on my literary scouting trips, which led me into the riverside world of animal rogues, dunces and innocents, and into the domain of wise, courageous and gentle folk. And with a child's imagination I located the characters and watched them playing their part in an enchanting tale.

I pursued The Three Men in their boat to a Cookham backwater, which the author called 'the sweetest stretch of all the river', and where he made the immortal trio step off and have tea. I dozed on the banks of the lazy-flowing Thames under willow-trees, close to whispering reeds and bulrushes. I watched the slow-motion river life from under a fringe of silver birches and elders, or sat by the stream in a meadow riotous with willow herb and crowfoot. And like Mole, I adjusted my senses to 'the sparkle, the ripple, the scents, the sounds and the sunlight', sometimes submerging my hand in the water, allowing my thoughts to float on his 'long, waking dream'.

I rambled through 'The Wild Wood', twigs crackling under my feet, looking out for fungus on tree stumps that resembled caricatures; I glanced over my shoulder, sensing menace, and steered clear of malice threatening behind trees that looked like 'dark reefs'. And at least once I thought I could hear the pit-a-pat of little feet and the voices of Messrs Toad and Badger.

Reluctantly I would return from such excursions into writers' fantasies, conscious of the gossamer thread between the child's world of make-believe and an adult world which tolerated only brief flights of escapism.

One Sunday morning, shortly after the garden party, the Canon entered my room with a knock and a breakfast tray.

Breakfast at the Vicarage had never been a family affair, partly because during the week Patricia left for London early, and on Sundays slept until the church bells drove her out of bed, partly because the Canon viewed breakfast like an ascetic, and on Sundays, before church, liked to go over his sermon again. 'You've been working hard all week,' he said. 'Let me spoil you a bit.'

The spoiling continued on Monday morning and for the rest of the week. However, the Canon's unbidden ministrations, which soon tempted him discreetly to narrow the physical space between us and – once talk about the day's weather had been exhausted – to fix his eyes on my face or pointedly study the intricate pattern on my nightdress, put me increasingly ill at ease. Most significantly so at an hour when the widower's lone black frame was not yet softened, nor his masculinity neutralized, by a white dog collar.

Another Sunday, and the good Canon sat down on my bed, uninvited, and slid a hand up my naked arm.

'How warm your skin is!'

But there was nothing paternal or pastoral about the gesture, nor about the flurry of excitement that rushed colour into the Canon's pale face. I shrank back into my pillows, repossessing my arm. Something snapped, sending a discordant note into the sunlit room. Sadness welled up behind my breastbone, and I knew that a good thing had ended. That the time had come to take my leave.

Patricia, who had not been blind to recent developments, and who, despite my denial, suspected her father of some unseemly approach, took the Canon angrily to task. For why else would I want to leave the vicarage so suddenly and at the height of summer? But I was not sure whether her fury was prompted by her father's reawakened sexuality so soon after her mother's death, or the agonizing thought that cooking dinner would now be incumbent upon her once more. She could, of course, also have realized in a flash of panic how near she had come to acquiring a German step-mother.

On the day of my departure I received a letter from the Matron of King's College Hospital, London, informing me that I had not been accepted as a pupil midwife. No reasons were given, but I knew whose reference was to blame. Though normally not given to uncharitable thought, I dispatched a curse in the direction of King Edward VII Hospital, and more specifically to a room in the main building, first floor up and left, second on the right.

And as if its news were meant to apply balm to my wounded ego, I received another letter.

'Just to let you know,' wrote Lotte, who was 'staffing' at King Edward's, 'there's been another theft of money from a nurse's room. But this time they caught the culprit, and she admitted to the earlier theft for which you got blamed. You'll be happy to know that your name has been cleared.'

The Canon had been right. Truth often took its time in clearing a person's reputation. But not always could it undo the harm false witness had done.

7

An alien in Berlin

Shortly before the train approached the specially constructed platform at the Soviet zonal frontier near Helmstedt, my fellow-travellers began to shift in their seats, and to display nervous symptoms more likely to be found in patients waiting in dental surgeries. Men and women who, bound by the common 'adventure' of crossing into Soviet-occupied territory, had chatted earlier about their flourishing post-war enterprises, the price of coffee or the whim of some in-law, grew suddenly tongue-tied. Some glanced surreptitiously at their suitcases on the rack or checked their papers again, others opened and shut purses or briefcases as in reflex actions. One man dried his palms with a handkerchief, another dabbed his forehead, a woman hid a parcel under her seat.

I was new to the phenomenon of anxiety gripping ordinary civilians at the thought of crossing into the Zone legally, and with no more identification required than a West German *Personalausweis*[1].

I was not new to the manifestations of fear.

As the train screeched to a halt, and stern-faced *Vopos*[2] and Soviet military reinforcements came into view, memories jumped back into my consciousness: trying to steal across the closed border into the Russian Zone in the harsh winter of 1946; lying prostrate in a frozen field under the first streaks of dawn, my face pressed against a nail-bed of stubble, while shots were ringing out over my head; staring at jackboots and an ankle-length Russian army coat, at a machine-gun trained at my head . . .

It had been seven days to Christmas, and all I had wanted was to reach Berlin and re-unite with my mother.

---

1 German identity card
2 East German police

Instant recollections of my second attempt the following spring: a goods train bound for Berlin, shunted on the eastern side onto a check-point track. Crouching on the floor of an empty driver's cabin, my head between my shoulders, I had been inches away from detection – from hands rattling the locks of sealed doors, and rifle barrels probing for stowaways; from the sound of heavy boots crunching over sleeper gravel, and of steely voices which, in a flash, returned memories of earlier days in Russian captivity. Angst pouring into my guts like molten metal, for minutes triggering off a bout of uncontrollable trembling – minutes during which I had wished I could make myself invisible . . .

Seven years had passed since.

The train stopped. *Vopos* noisily entered the carriage, emanating the authority of SS troopers and – judging by the look on their faces – loving every minute of their power of intimidation. And now I was back again in the wintry field and on the goods train.

A *Vopo* positioned himself before me, high-booted legs astride.

'Your papers!' he commanded. And after their close inspection, 'Where do you come from?'

'England.'

'Why are you travelling to Berlin?'

'To live with my mother.'

'Which part of Berlin?'

'British sector.'

'Open your suitcase!'

The *Vopo* went to work. As he found no porno magazines or literature blacklisted as being 'subversive' to the new Democratic State, and as Goethe's *Faust*, a collection of English Poetry, Shakespeare's Sonnets, an English Bible, a dictionary and the novels *Random Harvest* and *Rebecca* looked innocent enough, he returned my documents with a bored expression and proceeded to subject the other passengers to a similar scrutiny.

When the train finally moved out, there were sighs of relief all round, and hands, suddenly steadied, unwrapped sandwich parcels.

*   *   *

My mother met me at Bahnhof Zoo. With parts of its walls and its glass roof still missing, and although fully operational again, the station looked like an amputated giant. It reminded me of that fateful night in February 1945, when the adjoining city's zoo had been hit by several bombs, killing many animals and forcing cages open. For days, many a predator had been roaming the area in panic or in search of food, monkeys crouched in trees and freed reptiles, among them one reported anaconda, put the living fear into members of the rescue services.

In the station hall, once a place of German orderliness, where tickets were issued together with an unwritten guarantee for the punctual arrival and departure of trains, now an army of lost souls seemed to be whiling away the tristesse of their lives. Some, still dressed in shabby army coats, bore a deadly hue on their faces – the tell-tale sign of silicosis, contracted in Siberian mines from years of prisoner-of-war labour. A man on crutches. Painted prostitutes, swinging their hips and smiling speculative smiles. Boys, looking street-wise, cheated out of their child-hood. Spivs conducting some shady trade from vantage points, their hands discreetly exchanging currencies, their eyes, hawk-like, scanning the field for prospective customers or police presence.

The light in the hall was dim, the stone floor littered with paper and cigarette ends. For me, nothing seemed to have changed since my last brief visit less than two years after the war.

When I woke up next morning, there was, however, a surprise in store for me.

'Would you get some rolls for breakfast?' my mother asked.

For someone who still associated Berlin with the early post-war maize bread that had weighted the stomach like concrete, the crisp rolls made a delightful change from English white bread, and turned breakfast that morning in no less a feast than it had been five years ago on my first day at the Radcliffe.

I noticed other changes: the flat was centrally heated again, warm water ran from taps, the WC flushed and the electric light came on at whatever time one turned the switch. In the kitchen, a small refrigerator had replaced an ancient ice-box, and milk came in bottles, being no longer dispensed, as in my grandmother's time, from the urns of a horse-drawn dairy-van, or poured straight into the customer's jug for war-time coupons. There were white lace curtains at the windows, and the iron stove – the only source of warmth and only cooking facility in the bitterly cold winter of 1944–45 – had disappeared. Even the bomb damage on the dwelling's facade had been repaired.

In the streets, shop window displays overwhelmed me, and I stared in disbelief at the different cuts of meats and assortment of *wurst,* and at whatever had been in short supply or altogether absent from the consumer's table during the lean years. I pressed my nose against shop windows filled with the latest electrical appliances or with fashionable clothes; I keenly registered the number of private motor cars on the road, notably Volkswagen Beetles. And what firmer evidence was there that life in Berlin had resumed more than a modicum of normality than the sight of ladies wearing hats again, instead of headscarves, and showing off their legs in seamed nylons and high-heeled shoes. Men, too, were no longer wearing insignia-less grey tunics or frayed wartime suits, and many walked inches taller in crêpe shoes. Not so much, I was told, because the style was 'en vogue', but because men's feet, often having marched a thousand miles as soldiers or prisoners-of-war, were relishing the 'springy feeling of lightness' of such footwear.

Life on the streets of Berlin no longer ended at sunset, as it had done during the Blockade, and on the Kurfürstendamm, the city's once famous, pulsating avenue which, though mortally wounded, had refused to die in 1945, neon signs now advertised both old and new commercial brand names. Cinemas and theatres played to full houses, restaurants and night-clubs attracted a select clientele, among them the beneficiaries of the sterling and dollar exchange rates, as well as German entrepreneurs who, with a nose for post-war consumer needs, particularly in the housing sector, had jumped on to the band-waggon in good time and were now doing profitable business. Only at its upper end, the Kurfürstendamm was still waiting for that breath of life that would bring back shops and restaurants, customers and *flâneurs*[1].

Slowly, as I looked around the city, I saw the reverse of the picture. Prices were high, money for the average German in

1 Strollers

short supply. Magazines and newspapers spelled it out: since the economic recovery Berliners and West Germans had been riding high on the crest of several 'waves', each in turn being triggered off by the years of austerity and material loss. Initially, the *Fresswelle*[1] had carried people away, often to the point of gluttony, determined as they were to make up for the empty stomachs and cooking pots of yesterday. And such indulgence showed. Many men were loosening their belts again, and it seemed no coincidence that advertisements for ladies' whale-bone corsets swamped the market, no doubt catering for the army of housewives who crowded coffee-houses, gorging themselves with rich cream cakes topped, for good measure, with extra lashings of *Schlagsahne*[2].

Once stomachs had been satisfied and larders filled, the *Möbelwelle*[3] had driven people to acquiring new possessions, for only a lucky few had kept the roof over their heads or the contents of their homes. Furniture manufacturers and dealers did furious business, exploiting the common mood that security and a sound family life could only be found in a cosily furnished home, preferably equipped with modern gadgets and labour-saving devices.

'Buy, buy, buy,' cried the advertisements for toasters, radios and record-players, *Schlaraffia* mattresses, plastic goods, mini-cars, refrigerators and foam-rubber living-room comfort.

And it was only a matter of time before the chroniclers of German post-war indulgences spoke of the *Kleiderwelle*[4] breaking on consumers' shores. It was one trend no one but the thousands of refugees could afford to ignore. Perhaps understandably, the replacement of wartime garments had become an obsession, and from what I gathered in conversation with distant relatives, who had come through the war unscathed, new smart clothes provided instant status in a society in which the landed gentry, academics, aristocrats, bankers and wealthy business men had lost as much in the war as labourers and office clerks. A rich aunt gave me her version:

'New outfits help not only to distance one from the years of

1 (excessive) attention to food
2 Whipped cream
3 Furnishing and refurnishing trend
4 Clothes-buying trend

clothing coupons, but they also give one a new identity.'
Dress-makers, tailors and the fashion industry rubbed their hands.

Advertisements advocating that 'much deserved holiday' under an Adriatic or Mediterranean sun, finally launched the *'Reisewelle'*[1]. They also drove home to me the changes that had been going on while I had been away.

At the end of the second week I had been handed around on the social platter as the girl who had spent five years in England, training – of all things – as a nurse, and who had come back, preferring tea to coffee and praising English ways, and who was, would you believe it, sometimes searching for a German word!

I had coffee and Berliner apple cake with gentle folk who had remained lamentably insular in their outlook, and Boeuf Bourgignon with nouveau-riche Berliners, for whom the possession of a fondue set rated top in epicurial sophistication aids. Not being too sensitive in their dealings with the have-nots, and flying the German banner high, whatever its emblem, they told me outright over the sizzling copper bowl that they found me noticeably anglicized, and in my views alienated from good old German thinking.

I had open sandwiches and a glass of Moselle with twice-removed relatives who, with their middle-class comfort restored, and their door shut against the memory of Nazism and the war, seemingly still went to bed with Goethe, Hölderlin or Nietzsche in a world which, for them, the Lord be thanked, had resumed its former conceptional dimensions.

I accompanied a wealthy elderly uncle on a tour of Berlin's top night-clubs where, on saucer-sized dance-floors, couples moved to smoochy music, wine was astronomically priced and the waiters looked more gentlemanly than some of their customers.

And whether in dust-free drawing-rooms, at restaurant tables or in the streets, the city's peculiar geographical and political situation never failed to find critical analysts. At the end of the war, Berlin had been 'the city that refused to die'. Now, West Berliners spoke of their Western sectors as a 'political outpost of

---

1 Travelling trend

US imperialism', as 'Bonn's liability' or as 'West Germany's mistress'.

Uncle Hugo's vision went further. Financier, economist and rising entrepreneur in the construction business, he branded the 'victors' large-scale dismantling of German factories after the war as the drastic cure from which industry was rising like a Phoenix.

Meanwhile, I learned that there was no escape from rediscovered German values. Thematically flogged by latter-day moralists in the cinema, in magazines and advertisements, a return to orderliness, cleanliness, purity of body, nobility of mind and a heightened sense of family were being advocated. And nothing better reflected people's obsession with work, or fired them in their longings for security and the long-missed pleasures of life, than the slogan, *Freudig schaffen, freudig geniessen*[1], even if it bore an uncanny resemblance to the former Nazi motto, *Kraft durch Freude*[2].

One day I ventured into East Berlin, an experience which Western day-trippers had described as getting caught in a time warp.

Vopo presence at the checkpoint, uniforms, jackboots, pistols and unsmiling faces instantly intimidated the German visitor with memories of brutal, Russian-style policing. As I wandered through the heart of the Sector and some of its back streets, I grew increasingly despondent. A scene, I thought, worthy of a place in future history books: hastily erected new buildings towering over, or crouching beside ruins, graceless, style-less, homogenous with the severe, straight-line policies of the political system; shops displaying war-time dearth or shoddiness with a Communist price tag. Queues, drab Cafés, an absence of colour. And even more painful: pedestrians looking grey and silenced, often staring at the conspicuous Westerner with a mien suggesting an enforced prison mentality or, at best, the envy of the economically and politically impoverished for their infinitely better-off brothers and sisters from beyond the divide.

A few Wartburgs and Skodas were puttering about. And

---

1 'Enjoy your work, enjoy your leisure!'
2 'Strength through Joy'

wherever the eyes strayed, the stern poster images of Wilhelm Piek and Walter Ulbricht were watching passers-by in 'Big-Brothers' style, while flaking walls, pockmarked with bullet holes, screamed down slogans which hammered home the red tenet of political messages: East Berlin and the new Democratic Republic as part of an ideological bloc which demanded total submission and loyalty.

Unter den Linden, the once proud avenue which had seen emperors, Adolf Hitler and Russian tanks, as well as the cheerful, colourful crowds which had turned the city into a Metropole during the 1936 Olympic Games, now yawned with boredom, its ruins and plain-faced new edifices repelling the visitor in search of cherished landmarks. With a shock I realized that I was an alien in an alien city, a lost child abroad, who came out in goosepimples every time a Soviet military vehicle passed, or a Vopo looked at me, as if he were about to spot an enemy of the Republic. My sense of unease intensified as I approached the check-point on my way back, and I nearly bolted when an armed *Vopo* took time over the perusal of my identity card. And now, in broad August daylight, it was only common sense and a tight skirt, that kept me from sprinting across to the safety of the West.

That night I found nothing at all wrong with West Berlin in which democracy spelt freedom and lack of fear.

I might have got used to post-war German values, to Berliners preferring elbowing to orderly queuing at bus stops, to the arrogance of money and opinions, and to a coffee-and-cake *Gemütlichkeit*, during which conversation ranged from the merits of the latest washing powder to the versatility of kidney-shaped coffee-tables, or was limited to the city's insular, albeit all too vulnerable geographical position. I might have got used to Berlin, if during my social encounters with relatives and loosely defined friends of my mother's I had not met with a total lack of interest in England, the former enemy country, from which I had just returned. It puzzled me. For were people not enjoying peaceful slumber again? Were they not conscious of the comfort of a heated room, a plentiful table, a new wardrobe and members of the Allied Forces guarding their city's sectional border against communism? Could they not afford to be curious about England, of which teachers and Nazi propagandists had painted a distorted and often satirized picture? Could they not quiz me about her people, her landscapes and customs, or simply ask me what it had been like, working over there so soon after the war?

For me, such overt indifference suggested a stubborn provincialism, resentments not yet buried or mental attitudes that looked askance at anything un-German, or pointedly confined themselves to things German and proven to be indivisibly German.

At home, the adult in me found herself unable to build a bridge back to her childhood, which would have aided repatriation, and I resented my mother trying to make up for the lost years of home-making, by showering me with solicitude, if not clinging to my very presence like a child to its mother's apron strings.

Not surprisingly, torn between emotions, I failed to find a *modus vivendi* in a city which seemed to have sold its soul. In my worst moments I felt like a stranger in a land from which I had grown away, admittedly without much outside encouragement. My home-coming had flopped, it had rebounded. Even the initial culinary thrills of *Brötchen, wurst* and home-cooking were fading, and shops no longer lured me with their tantalizing displays. A new dress finally provided flickers of pleasure and a new mirror image. But when I suddenly started thinking in terms of new shoes, a new handbag, a new hair-style, and what a figure I would cut in the eyes of the neighbours, when, Deutschmarks and appearances on my mind, I cogitated about the adage *Kleider machen Leute*[1], the mocking face of materialism stuck out its tongue at me, and that inner voice, to which I had grown attuned over the years, and which had never failed me yet, warned me to keep clear of the whirlpool of surface values.

I ached for the England of Shakespeare, Pope and Tennyson, for spires, dreamy riverbanks, tea in mugs, cherry blossoms, steak pies, English hymns, wood-panelled libraries, queuing discipline, Sherlock Holmesian mists, people's 'Please' and 'Thank you' and the uplifting strains of Auld Lang Syne.

---

1 'Clothes made the man'

8

No sweet life in Merano

The Munich-Rome Express was steaming through the mountains of the Northern Tyrol, when my mother handed me carefully peeled, mouth-sized pieces of an apple on a paper napkin.

'How is your Italian coming on?' she asked.

'*Cameriere mi porti una bottiglia di vino rosso!*' I blurted out, rolling the 'r's and intonating each word with gusto. 'It means, "Waiter, bring me another bottle of red wine"!'

My mother smiled, and I returned my attention to the book which promised the mastery of *Basic Italian in One Week*.

For days, ever since a distant aunt had invited us to spend a holiday at her hotel in Merano, I had immersed myself in the study of useful verbs and phrases of the language. Even the bathroom had resounded from my conjugation of *essere*[1] and *avere*[1], and one night I had woken from a noisy dream, in which I was reeling off '*Io sono, tu sei, egli, ella è* . . .', as it had been French class practice in school.

'We shall shortly be in Bolzano,' announced my mother, and I was ready for my first question in Italian: '*Dov' è il binaro del treno per Merano?*'[2] Briefly, memories of a previous journey through northern Italy intruded upon my familiarization with Italian phrases. A train to Milano in 1942. A special carriage. Compartments filled with excitement and laughter. Germany's young sporting élite on their way to the European Athletic Youth Games, boys and girls in Hitler Youth uniforms, drilled for victory and good behaviour in the axis country. How thrilled I had been to be travelling abroad for the first time. How intently, once we had crossed the frontier, I had watched out for the first manifestations of 'foreignness', my nose pressed

---

1 'to be' and 'to have'
2 'From which platform does the train leave for Merano?'

against the compartment window . . .

'I wonder what *Tante* Paola looks like?' said my mother, who had never set eyes on the Signora. 'It was good of her to invite us. Perhaps she realizes that we have been through hard times.'

'It surely took her a long time to come to that conclusion,' I retorted, musing about the sudden gesture of hospitality from a twice-removed aunt who had not bothered to keep in contact with her German relatives. But then I knew about the indolence of good intentions, and I was prepared to greet the *Tante* as a benefactress who, before her time was up, was perhaps prompted by a Christian desire to perform a good deed.

The Hotel Maria stood in a delightful, elevated position in the Maya Alta district of Merano, where many hotels were located. As a concession to southern style, its façade was ochre-coloured and each room boasted a small balcony with ornamental iron railings.

'*Buon giorno!*' said *Tante* Paola, a short and full-bosomed lady who wore her cloud of grey hair swept up in the fashion of Kaiser Wilhelm's time. Her dark clothes, relieved only by a white crocheted collar, pointed to a disregard for modern fashion trends and fitted admirably into the dusty Imperial Austrian atmosphere of the hotel.

In the high-ceilinged, corniced dining-room, which looked out on to a garden and mountain scenery, I half-expected archdukes and other titled guests to ladle their *brodo* or remove the flesh from the bones of a *pollo arrosto* with an understatement of motions, while coping aesthetically with the long strands of pasta or sauerkraut.

'Ah, and this is Marianne!' the *Tante* stated flatly, looking me up and down as if assessing my labour potential or my in-law suitability.

I stared at the large bunch of keys on a chain which she carried fastened to her belt, and which suggested a mistrust of, if not an uncomfortable relationship, with her Italian staff.

'I have to keep everything under lock and key,' she explained, as if she had read my mind. 'They would steal my dentures if I left them lying about. But tell me, what is life in Berlin like these days?' And without waiting for the visitors' account, 'I'm afraid, I won't be seeing much of you, my dears. We're fully booked until the end of November.'

Though spacious, our room faced north and suffered from the added gloom of an overhanging terrace. But outside, late August was bathing Merano in warm sunshine, luring *Kurgäste*[1] to Merano's promenades and public gardens, where elderly musicians, ensconced on band-stands, played sprightly tunes by Strauss and Léhar – music to stroll by, music to idle away the hours.

On shady coffee-house terraces, in a stage-setting of delicious *ennui,* grey-haired gentlemen with distinctive features, watch-chains, straw hats and white breast-pocket handkerchieves were reading newspapers or wallowing in their cogitations over a glass of wine, while their ladies, impeccably dressed and coiffured, aged complexions hidden under wide-brimmed hats, gingerly forked their way through *Sachertorte* and sipped coffee like communion wine. Every now and then, lorgnettes or monocles went into action, inspecting passers-by or whatever caught the myopic attention of patrons.

On the flower-lined promenade, gentlemen strollers leaned heavily on silver-topped walking-sticks or swung them like youthful dandies. Octagenarians displayed the bearing of field-marshals or royalty, while ladies of indeterminate age and understated elegance, unaccompanied, or lagging a step or two behind their husbands, talked in thin soprano voices to their poodles or Pekineses. And the dogs, perhaps conscious of pedigree, a bejewelled collar or a studded leather lead, knew better than to bark or sniff or lift a hind leg in a scenario in which timelessness and old-world refinement were of the essence.

Indeed, time seemed to have by-passed Merano, to have stopped its clock some time before the outbreak of the first world war. This was in no small way reflected by the picturesque, arcaded and sleepy streets in the old quarter of the town, where life dictated its own charming pace. Once the favourite resort of the Austrian and German aristocracy taking the grape cure in autumn and 'the waters' in spring, Merano had to all appearances come through the war like a backwoods village. Its mountain torrents still thundered down alongside

---

1 Visitors in a spa

groomed walkways, to join the Adige tributaries, its vineyards still soaked up the sunshine, and its light-bodied, fruity wine and *Traubensaft*[1] were still advocated as a panacea for more than physical ills.

In full harmony with the place, my mother and I ambled along the famous *Tappeiner Weg* and drank grape juice like water. We visited Bolzano, the town bordering on to the stupendous scenery of the Dolomites. We slept long, had wine with dinner and gorged ourselves with grapes and peaches. In the evenings we played Rommé, unless I practised conversational Italian on an elderly couple from Verona. At the end of the first week my mother started wondering how long we could decently stay at the Hotel Maria as non-paying guests. But although gifting us with fleeting smiles, *Tante* Paola remained unavailable for a chat. Forever busy, phoning, dealing with guests or doing her accounts, forever on the move, unlocking and re-locking linen cupboards, larder and winestore, if not supervising room-maids, kitchen and dining-room staff, she often seemed to be in two places at a time, not one grey hair out of place, and an impressive cameo brooch clasped at her neck like a badge of authority.

'I'll see you tonight, meine Lieben,' she would call out in passing, but once dinner was over, and the guests settled in the lounge, she stayed firmly incommunicado, leaving the reception desk and drinks service to a consumptive-looking waiter.

On the tenth day she called my mother and me into her parlour, a room heavy with velvet, lace, antimacassars and turn-of-the-century furniture. She did not smile, neither did she ask us to sit down, which degraded my mother and made me feel like a school-girl summoned to the headmistress for some misdemeanour.

'The two of you have enjoyed my hospitality for some time now,' she began. 'I hope you slept well.'

'Thank you,' said my mother, 'very well indeed.'

'And you enjoyed our food?'

'We did indeed. You have an excellent cook.'

'And there was enough of it?'

---

1 Grape juice

'Oh, yes, plenty.'

My mother was about to enumerate the pleasures Merano and the Hotel Maria had to offer their visitors, when the *Tante* cut her short.

'Don't you think then the time has come for Marianne to earn your board and lodging?'

My mother face fell. 'What do you mean, Paola?'

The *Tante* did not suffer my mother's incomprehension lightly. Impatience curled the corners of her mouth.

'I told you you could both stay as my guests for a while, in return for which I would expect Marianne to lend me a hand. We're in the middle of the busy autumn season. I'm short of staff, and my own health . . . '

By now the colour had left my mother's face and she was swallowing hard.

'You never wrote anything about Marianne working for our holiday,' she said.

'Oh, yes, I did,' countered the *Tante,* and not giving my mother time to recover her pride, she addressed herself to me.

'Have you got a job waiting in Berlin?'

I shook my head.

'Well then, you could start tomorrow. Come down at seven, young lady, and I'll show you the ropes. I'm afraid it'll mean long hours during the season, but you may have the early afternoon hours off, to be with your mother.'

Lost for words, I merely nodded agreement and stared out of the window at an unfolding day which no longer evoked a holiday spirit.

For my mother, the generous allocation of a few hours to spend with her daughter, settled the issue.

'Under the circumstances, Paola, I shall not remain under your roof any longer,' she said. 'Marianne may well stay on until our holiday stay is paid off. But I don't mind telling you that I find your assumption very strange. You didn't even hint at such an arrangement in your letter.'

'Oh, yes, I spelled it out to you quite clearly, *meine Liebe,*' retorted the *Tante.* 'I thought I was doing you a favour. I understand you're living on a widow's pension. I'm afraid I can't afford to run a charity institution . . . two adults staying for ten days on full board. You must understand.'

My mother pulled me out of the room. She did not slam the door, as she must have felt inclined to do, but allowed it to shut softly. Back in our room, she started crying with humiliation. My moment had come.

'I don't mind staying on and learning something about the hotel business,' I said by way of consolation. 'It'll also give me a chance to improve my Italian.'

My mother dried her tears.

'*Ach, mein Kind*, you're always seeing the bright side of things.'

Next morning she returned to Berlin.

As befitted my new status as an unpaid employee, I was told to move to the servants' quarters in the attic. Mean-sized and uncarpeted, my new room was furnished with a creaky bed, a wobbly wardrobe and a rickety stand supporting an earthenware basin and water jug. But then, sunshine was streaming through the window which afforded a spectacular view across Merano and the Adige valley to the distant blue hues of the Dolomites.

With a sudden levity of spirit I reported to *Tante* Paola for work on the stroke of seven. I had, after all, scrubbed floors before, washed dishes, sorted dirty laundry, cleaned rooms and served at table. The years in England had been stern task masters. They had taught me to see the world through a worm's eyes, and to tackle jobs alien to my nature or inclinations, offensive to my pride or my senses.

A surprise was in store for me.

The *Tante* heaved a sigh, gave me a wide smile and took me by the hand like a fairy godmother.

'Come,' she said, 'I'll show you how to run a hotel. It'll take you a few days to get the knack of it, but you're intelligent, and I heard you speaking some Italian.' She handed me a set of keys. *Ecco*, a token of my trust. Look after them well. Never forget to lock a cupboard. And now, let's start with the kitchen and the larder.'

Two weeks later I had fashioned myself confidently into my new role, devoting energy and common sense to every chore and dealing with kitchen hands, room maids and waiters with a quiet authority which, I had to admit, was significantly boosted by the power of a heavy bunch of keys conferred on me. October stole into Merano through the back door. Temperatures remained mild, the force of the northern winds being broken by the mountains. The sun continued to shine generously, but less fiercely, mountain peaks no longer hid behind a haze, and the air, though still loaded with fragrance, had the freshness of alpine streams. Peaches were juicier, grapes sweeter, and the locals pronounced their regional wines to be maturing well in body and character. At the hotel I supervised dining-room staff and helped at table whenever my services were required. I handed out fresh bed linen and towels, inspected rooms and renewed flowers in vases. I prepared hors d'hoeuvres and dished out desserts. I learned to prepare *zabaglione* from egg yokes, sugar, beaten egg whites and whipped cream, laced with Marsala – a fluffy dream which had me scrape the bowl and lick the spoon. Much of my time in the kitchen was spent unlocking and relocking the larder, for cook had to ask me for every egg, every pint of milk, every ounce of flour and sugar, the table waiters for every bottle of wine, to be issued on the production of a signed order slip. *Tante* Paola, I thought, was taking no chances.

I also received new guests, dealt with the formalities of arrivals, with police checking the guest-book and passports and, by letter or telephone, with bookings. I carried luggage to rooms, whenever the porter was doubling up as gardener. In the evenings, when *Tante* Paola remained invisible, I manned the reception desk, brought up bottles of wine and often stayed up until the last guests had retired. Some couples, curious about the *proprietària* entrusting me with so much responsibility and demanding all-round duties from one so young, might ask me to join them in the lounge for a chat or to make up a threesome for Rommé over a bottle of Traminer, while one night, an elderly French *comte*, a gentleman of acquiline features and patrician manners, asked me to go to bed with him as politely and charmingly as if to accompany him for an after-dinner stroll.

I became friendly with a newly-wed couple – an Englishman who had been managing a South American ranch for many years, and his German wife, Irene, who had been discharged recently from a TB sanatorium. By the time the happy and *simpatico* couple left, I knew about their plan to settle on the island of Mallorca for climatic reasons and we had exchanged addresses.

Contrary to my expectations *Tante* Paola allowed me to share her table in her private dining-room, around which there would assemble an ailing sister who spent most of her time bent over embroidery, a visiting brother who was suffering from dermatitis and taking 'the cure', and a diminuitive female cousin who, in the style of poor relatives, was earning her keep by mending the hotel linen.

Main meals served at the family table consisted, with few variations of Tyrolean *wurstl con krauti, pollo* or *vitello,* preceded by *pasta* cooked *al duro* and served either with blobs of fresh butter and Parmesan cheese or – since *Tante* Paola came from Genoa – with *pesto,* a local sauce containing basil, cheese, garlic and pine nuts. And there were always the desserts to look forward to: sweet almond cakes, puddings doused with caramel sauce, or my favourite, *zabaglione,* following which offers of sun-drenched fruit formed as natural an end to a meal as an 'Amen' to prayer.

Late autumn's gentle climate persisted through to November, if under a steadily diminishing sun, drawing able-bodied hill-walkers and those late-season holidaymakers who, once daylight was gone and the first keen winds blew down from the mountains, liked to sit in one of the cosy *Weinstuben* in the old quarter over a glass of local wine.

'Let me explain the books to you,' said *Tante* Paola one morning and proceeded to give me an intensive course in two-ledger book-keeping and the making out of bills. A few days later she informed me that she was going to Munich for a week for a specialist medical examination, and that she was leaving me 'in charge'.

The sudden shouldering of full responsibility was no small feat for me. However, with my fast-growing Italian vocabulary and an ear for its tuneful flow, with the staff marvelling at my ability to converse in four languages, if not as often being in two places at a time, just like the Signora, nothing untoward happened while the *Tante* was away. Guests kept arriving and leaving, none complained and all paid their bills. Supervising meals, I made sure that the service did not slacken and the waiters did not spill the consommé. When the *Tante* returned, she patted me on the back and expressed her satisfaction by giving me a whole day off.

Looking at her through the eyes of a qualified nurse, I noticed a new pallor on her face, behind which her personality appeared somewhat deflated. Gone was her domineering presence, before which staff had bowed and diners tried not to stain the table cloth. Even her pace had slowed down and her voice dropped to a lower key.

'Carry on as if I were still away, Marianne,' said the *Tante*, no more than glancing at the books and even leaving me to discuss the day's menu with the cook. At her own table, talk was now noticeably subdued and often replaced by the clinking of cutlery and plates, just as if someone in the family had died.

I gave no thought to returning to Berlin. Cheap labour I might have been, but I was enjoying myself in a job which provided useful practical and human experiences and promoted self-confidence. And once again I acknowledged my self-styled dictum that no matter what one was doing in life, it was preferable, and not without rewards, to do it to the best of one's ability.

Two weeks later the hotel closed. Seasonal staff were paid off and dust sheets spread over the upholstery. Outside, strong winds and rain showers marked an abrupt change of season.

'It's time you went home, Marianne,' said *Tante* Paola. 'You've done very well and I am grateful. I doubt whether I could have managed without you.' She opened her purse and extracted several one-thousand lire notes.

'Here, take this, girl. Buy yourself something nice. I'll be off to Munich again in a day or two. I'm booked into a clinic . . . '

My face must have registered compassion and question marks. Perhaps the *Tante* also realized that she owed me the truth.

'I have cancer, Marianne,' she said quietly.

I remembered how meticulously she had tidied her desk, ripping up letters and papers. How, only yesterday, I had found her, staring out of the window at a scene now bereft of the loveliness of spring and summer, the mellowness of autumn.

Impulse made me take the *Tante*'s hands. My eyes deputized for my voice.

'*Cara mia*,' she said, a maternal smile flitting across the spinster's face, before she squared her shoulders and looked at some distant spot like a general at an enmy army.

Just then the telephone rang, and I rushed towards it as if it formed the only sane connection with the outside world.

'*Pronto!*' I said, and told the Italian caller at the other end that the hotel had closed for the winter.

That afternoon I went into town and bought myself a real leather handbag and a pair of matching leather gloves.

'*Addio!* Marianne,' said the *Tante,* when I took my leave. She did not say '*Arrivederci!*' or '*Auf Widersehen!*'. Did she know that she would never return to her hotel, nor to her beloved *Maya Alta*?

9

Roses at my bedside

The first Christmas trees were on sale in Berlin's street markets, shop windows dazzled with their festive displays of goods. In department stores shoppers rubbed elbows, newspapers spoke of the trade as doing brisk seasonal business and delicatessens took orders for Christmas fare from gourmets not intimated by prices, and from the western city's nouveau-riche for whom a *Rollenhagen*[1] five-course menu or a cold buffet held undisputed status value. The *Kurfürstendamm* was teeming with vitality, but behind it my powers of recall saw more: a nightmarish stretch of a boulevard. Life lumbering on between smouldering ruins and cavernous buildings. Bowls of watery cabbage soup, cooked over iron stoves, being sold to the hungry. Remaining film theatres offering *Heimatfilme*[2] or happy-end romances as morale boosters to a worn-out, starving and freezing population which Hitler had urged, no, commanded, to resist the 'Bolshevist hordes'. Christmasses blessed, for a few days and nights, with death-less skies, and giftless but for those 'little things' made from the remains of cardboard, glue, paint, felt or yarn. Christmasses, when a few candles, a sparsely decorated tree and a handful of *pretzels*, baked with the most modest of saved-up ingredients, had formed the festive background to the strains of 'Silent Night, Holy Night'. These had perhaps delivered the Christmas spirit more faithfully in accord with the Scripture than it was now being hailed under a festoon of lights and in what appeared to me an obsession to make up, in the volume, size and costliness of gifts, for the material paucity of the wartime years. And already voices were pleading for a return to a less materially-orientated celebration of the *Fest*[3], and social analysts saw the existing trend as an obsessional

---

1 famous city delicatessen and party delivery service
2 sentimental films in idealized regional setting
3 Christmas

severance from wartime values.

For me, Christmas 1953 was different in more than one sense. Returning from Merano, I found myself again at a loose end and, as on previous occasions, hankering for new horizons. As German customs and manners threatened to reclaim their birthright, I tried to keep the fire of my Anglomania burning, by training my sights on British shores. I fed my appetite for the English language with second-hand paperbacks, which looked as if they had been retrieved from GI's trash cans, and nourished my love for English Literature, by sojourning into the world of poetry. I rambled with the Romantics, struggled through Matthew Arnold's *Rugby Chapel* and learnt by heart the last stanza of *Dover Beach*; I soaked up messages from Milton's *On His Blindness* and *God's Purposes Revealed*, and became a willing philosopher's pupil in Shakespeare's *All the World is a Stage*. And looking westwards across the Channel, geographically and mentally, I was prepared to sell my loyalties to anything that vaguely smacked of being English or British. I was, however, unable to ignore the need for a paying job.

Nursing in German hospitals did not appeal to me, not only because the profession afforded *Schwestern* too low a status, by admitting young women with no more than a statutory education, but because I would have come up against a different training structure, and a job concept which concentrated mainly on bedside nursing. Nor was I keen to opt for a life in which strict vocational principles and a white-corridor regime culti-vated mental attitudes and personal images more likely to be found in a religious order. One interview had sufficed.

'I see you trained in England.' A long pause. The formidable *Oberin*[1], a cross between a Mother Superior and a prison wardress, looked at me as if I were an alien intent on infiltrating her staff with 'foreign' ideas and practices.

'We prefer to train our own nurses. Any outsider would first have to adjust to our system and, like the rest of our nurses, be prepared to undertake domestic ward duties. How long did you say you've been away from Germany?'

I had heard enough. I remembered Lotte's assessment of the scope of German nurses: 'They're not allowed to do half the clinical work for which they train us over here. Why do you

---

1 'O' level (grade) Latin

think I chose to come to England?'

In sounding out my prospects for the immediate future, I gave up any hope of ever resuming my nursing career in England. King Edward's unforgiving Matron would surely see to it, by virtue of an acerbic reference, that I remained effectively barred from re-entering the country on a nurse's contract. What a price to pay for my inopportune smile outside Westminster Hall, and for my looks which – what a disgrace! – had once attracted the attention of the Surgical Registrar!

Temporarily I toyed with the idea of continuing my education at university level, but any attempt to gain admission faltered under the post-war regulations of German universities bent on re-establishing themselves as the towers of learning. Under the new rules, candidates, who had passed their *Abitur* after 1942 were no longer eligible for matriculation, and required to re-sit principal school subjects again. Too many teaching hours, the high-priests and restorers of academic excellence insisted, had been wasted through prolonged school holidays, during which the Hitler Youth had sent the upper classes to work on farms or run rural kindergartens. Too many hours of study had been lost through daytime air-raids, Hitler Youth meetings and Party collection schemes. Why, Nazi educationalists had even brought the *Abitur* exams conveniently forward by as much as three months, in order to draft school leavers into war service. And universities stood firm: entry standards were raised to 'acceptable' levels, and prospective Modern Languages students were required to produce evidence of having passed the 'Small *Latinum*'[1].

For me, the lack of funds decided matters. Not only a desire to contribute to the housekeeping, but also for the kind of financial independence that would enable me to rent a furnished room where I could escape from my mother's long, loving, possessive arms, from a love that would have liked me to regress to childhood dependence, and which now tried to chain me to her own mental and physical boundaries.

Chance pointed to the British Military Hospital in Berlin. I applied and was immediately accepted as a State Registered Nurse, to work under Q.A.R.A.N.C.[1] sisters.

1 Queen Alexandra Royal Army Nursing Corps

For once, the arm of King Edward's Matron had not been long enough.

The hospital, a former German police training school, stood in leafy surroundings on the outskirts of Spandau, a small historic town bordering on the Russian Zone. Like Spandau prison, which was housing the last of the Nuremberg war criminals, and like the former *Wehrmacht* barracks, which was now home to British troops, the BMH commanded a solid presence in the British Sector of Berlin.

The effort of getting to work each morning amounted to no less than self-flagellation. For it required all my will-power to rise in the cold, small hours of the morning, when dawn was still many winks of sleep away, and mind and body performed like robots.

At 5.15 my alarm clock hammered metal against metal.

'Wake up,' my mother would cry from her bed, when I had silenced the instrument of torture and turned over for those blissful extra minutes of sleep, which are as sweet as the sudden release from pain. Time would be ticking over, but not for long. For suddenly it would drum each second into my reluctant consciousness. And now it was a sleep-walk to the bathroom, a hasty bowl of porridge, an even hastier cup of tea, then a sprint to the suburban five-forty-five, through streets still steeped in winter darkness. Two changes of trains. Freezing, wind-exposed platforms sticking out of a whitish, slow-waking urban landscape like concrete islands. Finally, a tram ride, followed by a five-minute walk under the hesitant streaks of dawn. A quick change into uniform.

'Good morning Sister!'

'Good morning, Nurse!'

The clock struck seven. I was back on familiar ground, yet a newcomer to a world within a world run to military protocol, a stranger to a self-governing, self-sufficient body of administrative, medical and nursing staff, which came complete with its own cooks, clerks, chaplains, ambulance drivers, porters, maintenance men, guards and staff manning, or supervising, canteens, store-rooms, the pharmacy and a field post office. Supplied with British Army food, from garden peas to tinned prunes and tomato ketchup, and effectively fenced off at its perimeter by brick walls, barbed wire and a guard-room, this

British blot on Spandau soil tended and jealously protected its insularity under its Union Jack.

With the exception of a midwife, who had lived and worked in South African hospitals for many years, all German nurses had British SRN qualifications. Clinical procedures did not differ from those 'back home', neither did drugs and medicines, measuring units, the size and shape of bedpans, the geometry of bed-making. Only the working pace was slower, emergencies less frequent, bed occupancy lower, and the number of male patients outnumbered that of hospitalized women and children, known as 'dependents'. Most noticeably, there was no hierarchical division of nursing duties, and if anything reminded me of breathing German air, it was the percolated *Jacobs* coffee which we prepared in the ward kitchen for 'elevenses', and the fresh *Berliner* rolls which some obliging soul fetched for the German staff every morning.

The New Year arrived with snow showers and bleak skies filtering reluctant daylight on to urban streets. The hours I spent away from home now left little time for leisure. I never got back before seven at night, and after *Abendbrot*[1] I felt little inclined to go out and explore what life had still in store for me. My alarm clock, wound up, its waking finger pointing to an hour when the gods were still asleep, would soon lure me to bed.

'Why don't you move into the dormitory?' a nurse asked. 'You'd get heaps more sleep – and more freedom.'

I packed a suitcase and moved into the hospital attic, in which four bedroom cells were sectioned off by plywood screens and curtains, and furniture was limited to a bed, a chair and a clothes line.

I was to share the attic with another German nurse.

Nurse A. was known to be very popular with male hospital staff. Voluptuously built, and speaking in the rough Berlin patois, her nursing uniform barely disguised her sexual appetite and her availability. Off-duty, with make-up plastered on, and

---

1 Supper

her lascivious tongue finding no subject taboo, she bore an uncanny resemblance to King Edward's one-time nurse of horizontal repute, sharing such distinction with Fifi, the Belgian whore who, at one stage of my 'naked years', had briefly been propelled into my life with her companion.

Hardly had I gone to bed the first night, indulging in the luxurious prospect of extended sleep, when the door creaked open. Female whispers mingled with male chuckles, stockinged feet stole to the bed just beyond the flimsy partition and only inches from my ear. Two bodies crept noisily into an embrace, whereupon groaning bed springs and a *sotte voce* duet of little yelps and grunts recorded the progress of physical activity. Finally, an orgastic cheer resounding from the rafters proclaimed that the sexual mountaineers had reached their Everest.

Not long afterwards, there came the sound of swishing clothes, legs struggling into trousers, bare feet making painful contact with a chair and tip-toeing towards the door. Then it grew quiet in the attic but for a contented snore. In my bed, chaste and wide awake, I listened to the excited language of my body, which the stroke of midnight would finally subdue.

The next night I was not surprised to hear my dormitory mate and her male protagonist playing another 'Act for Two'. But now I detected a variation in the fugue of lusty sounds and the bass nuance in the male voice, while on the third night, the stealthy wooer established himself in my mind not only as being of heftier build, but also horizontally more agile than his predecessors. Finally, having woken on three mornings with my eyes leaden with sleep and my body feverish from the night's obtrusive images and sound effects, I longed for fresh air and privacy, for a place where the corrupting voices of promiscuity could not find a physical echo. Where I could catch up with my dreams – dreams that featured love, not lust.

I phoned my mother.

'Mutti, I'm coming home again.'

I had been working for several weeks on the Officers' Ward, when the window of one room was fitted with bars, patients were moved to a lower floor, and the two staircases leading to the Officers' Ward were closed to all traffic. Armed guards were posted at doors and on stairways, guard-room personnel was doubled. A cleaning brigade got busy on the Officers' Ward, supervised by Military Police. Two Q.A.R.A.N.C. Sisters established themselves in the ward office, while German staff, myself included, were transferred to the Female Wards. 'A temporary measure,' they said, not giving any reasons, and opening the door wide to speculations. For judging by the elaborate security arrangements, no lesser patient than a visiting Head of State could be expected.

One sunny morning, an Army cavalcade brought an ambulance close to the main entrance of the Male Wards. Out stepped a thin, grey-haired man who, stooping slightly, and glancing furtively about, was hastily ushered inside. That was all I saw of the VIP patient – the former Admiral Doenitz, one of the prisoners tried at Nuremberg and serving his sentence at Spandau prison.

'Why top security for someone who looked as if the sound of a bugle could topple him?'

'The Soviets insisted,' the military pundits explained. 'They're afraid he might be kidnapped by former Nazis or German right wing extremists.'

'A political operetta,' declared my uncle, calmly draining his glass of Riesling. 'The poor bastard is nothing but a pawn in a game between the Soviets and the Allies.'

Spring saw me in a furnished room in Charlottenburg, which reduced my commuting time and distanced me from my mother's life in which, as a prisoner of love and attention, I felt my own growth being retarded. The light-footed, sweet-smelling season also plunged me into a social whirlpool of tentative and unstable relationships which from afar bore the promise of romance, but at close quarters turned out to be just another variation on the *cherchez-la-femme* theme, or which, still in the bud, or just short of the blossoming stage, proved too risky, too degrading, too fragile or unacceptable, for me to indulge in, or to hope for consistency.

A dashing British Army surgeon took me out to dinner in a smart restaurant on the *Kurfürstendamm*, where the waiters bowed to his Captain's uniform as if he were royalty. Over roast venison and a bottle of *Chateau-Neuf-du Pape*, my ostenatious flirt talked about the frailty of the male ego, and about husbands whose wives, in their last months of pregnancy, were focussing their attention on their unborn babies, while assigning their husbands, figuratively-speaking, to bread and water in their nuptial beds.

I sighed compassion. 'How many children have you got?'

'Two,' my date said, and called for the bill.

Later, manoeuvred into a dark hallway and into a vulnerable position, I fought the captain's renewed ardour with blunt realism.

'What about your wife?' I asked. 'What if she were to go unexpectedly into early labour in your absence, with your present whereabouts unknown?'

Shocked by my unromantic observations into instant emotional sobriety, the captain tried to save his officer and gentleman's face, putting space between us and his lips to my hand.

'You're right, Marianne. Forgive me. The wine . . ., ' he sighed. 'But how easily I could fall in love with you . . . '

Needless to say, I was not invited out for dinner again.

A British government official and former patient treated me to an expensive luncheon at the *Pfälzer Weinstuben*. Armed with the finest Lindt chocolates, smooth talk and polished manners, he tried to navigate me into the acquiescent waters of an affair. His charm, his clothes were impressive, the expertise with which he courted me under the eyes of attentive waiters over a heavy Palatinate wine and the first cream-whipped strawberries of the season, were worthy of a diplomat. Not so the handling of the crucial moment.

Having taken me home, he switched off the engine and glanced at his watch. A warm hand cupped my knee. Compliments. A smile schooled and seductive, suggesting a little afternoon infidelity. Not for him the classical statement, 'My wife doesn't understand me', or 'My wife prefers to read "The Fall of the Roman Empire" in bed'. No, just a flat request: 'May I come up with you?'

I tore myself free and jumped out of the sleek car. I think I slammed the door. And just in time I remembered my manners.

'Thank you very much for a lovely lunch,' I said to the man at the wheel, my smile as sweet as the chocolates in the box under my arms. I felt very mean.

I was dated by an American officer and physicist from Albuquerque, who dined and wined me at the US Press Club in *Zehlendorf*. We talked across candlelight and over French champagne and T-bone steak: Hitler and the war, Marlene Dietrich, Californian oranges, The Bible, The Bomb, and man's inherent loneliness. We talked about Heine, the poet and saddened emigrant, which made my darkly handsome escort recite, '*Ich weiss nicht, was soll es bedeuten, dass ich so traurig bin* ...'

Then we talked about love.

At the coffee and liqueur stage, our conversation suddenly stopped. Our eyes locked, our smiles dropped, the candle-light flickered. Between us, even the air seemed to vibrate.

My companion's voice wrapped itself around me like velvet.

'I feel we have known each other for a long time. How I wish I were staying longer in Berlin. I'm afraid my business here is almost finished, and I reckon I'll be going back to the States in a week or two. And now, here you are, Marianne, and I'm desperately trying not to fall in love with you.'

Later that night, my armour, my frustrations, my loneliness melted away. In my partner's arms I asked no questions, I demanded nothing, I gave no thought to the morrow ...

'What are you smiling about?' asked a nursing colleague next morning. 'You look like a cat what's just licked cream!'

I stared out of the window at the sky, in which racing, shifting clouds conveyed a strong sense of impermanence. Yet although I undersood their message, although I knew that there were no concessions to fatigue, however sweet, I was unable to wipe that smile off my face.

And then came the night when I went to bed without *Abendbrot*, my insides raw with the pain of parting and loneliness restored. But even then, I think, my face held a hint of a smile.

The Berlin Ball season was in full swing, Ludwig, a solicitor asked me to accompany him to the Lawyers and Solicitors' Annual Gala Dance. I wore my first long dress and drank champagne like orange squash. I danced all night, and with other revellers ended up at five in the morning in the *Holländische Kaffeestube* for a breakfast of piping hot bouillon, coffee, succulent ham, and *Brötchen* fresh from the baker's oven.

'My mother would like to meet you, Marianne. What about coming for afternoon coffee next Sunday?' Ludwig sounded charmingly conventional and alarmingly serious at this sobering hour, when all I had on my mind was how I was going to get through another working day at the B.M.H. without falling asleep on the ward.

Luckily, my emotions were not galloping away with me. For in the weeks to come, at parties or in the company of Ludwig's best friends, I heard my blue-eyed suitor answering to the name of 'Lulu'. The odd smirk, veiled hints and the strange glint in the eyes of one male eventually drove home to me the message that Lulu's beauty did not appeal to the female sex alone. My naive understanding of sexual partnerships was shattered, as I realised that Ludwig dallied in both camps. How much I still had to learn about the human circus, in which macho men, trapeze artists, freaks of nature and gentle clowns performed side by side.

Summer came to Berlin. Women were wearing short-sleeved dresses, doutdoor cafés were crowded, and the white Havel sand backing on to the pine-scented *Grundewald* ran warm and dry through one's fingers.

I met R., and now spent many a warm Sunday, boating on the Havel lakes, many a Saturday night at the 'Oasis' nightclub on *Kurfürstendamm*, where the *borsch* soup was reputed to be the finest outside Russia. Where Russian immigrants played balalaikas and sonorous voices sang the songs of Mother Russia, while the dancers' boots stamped wildly to the passion of the music. Where the song 'Kalinka' made the vodka-drinkers clap their hands and often enough carried even those away who were drinking whisky or *Liebfrauenmilch*.

R. was an enigmatic, taciturn Scot who did not suffer fools gladly. His back and shoulders betrayed the four years he had spent in East Prussia in a PoW camp, felling trees and working in the fields. Although he lacked the physical and mental attributes of the men for whom I had so easily fallen in the past, and although, emotionally and culturally, we stood light years apart, I was drawn to him, slowly, inexorably and against all reasoning, perhaps because we had met at the roadside inns of our lives.

R. was also a kind man, reliable, generous and of an easy-going disposition. He made me laugh. He brought stability into my life. He was a bachelor.

In his arms I finally found peace and an 'English' refuge.

Summer was at its height when my health took a series of nasty bends, just as if by laying me low for some time a compulsory analysis of my life would help me to set my sights on the future. Over several months my social calendar had left neither time, nor room for that essential loneness in which thoughts will mature. I had been playing hard, dancing to many a tune, and often losing my footing on the slippery ground of relationships.

One morning, following days of indigestion, I woke to a feeling of nausea and utter misery in my belly. In the bathroom, I looked in disgust a my tongue in the mirror and vomited. I rang the GP's surgery.

'I'm sorry,' said the receptionist, 'the doctor can't call before noon. We've got a heavy patient load this morning.'

By mid-morning, my temperature had risen, and I felt as if a deadly fungus was growing in my abdomen. A taxi drove me to the surgery.

'I've got appendicitis,' I said. 'May I see the doctor.'

The receptionist smiled indulgently, and I read her thoughts: 'Fancy, patients diagnosing their own ailments!'

'I know what I'm talking about,' I insisted. 'I'm a trained nurse.'

This revelation worked. The doctor saw me at once, examined me, reached for the phone and called an ambulance. Less than an hour later I was on the operating table.

'It was a close shave,' said the surgeon, when I came to. 'Blessed appendix was about to burst. A matter of minutes. Would have been a messy affair . . . '

That evening, R. visited me with a big bunch of red roses.

On my return to work I was temporarily put in charge of the Officers' Ward where life had returned to normal. My first task was to turn a room into an isolation ward, and admit a mother of four, who was suffering from meningitis. My fellow-nurses and I wore cap and gown, when attending to the patient, and we took all routine precautions until isolation restrictions were lifted. When the patient was finally discharged from hospital, the room was thoroughly disinfected. But there would come the day when I would probe my memory for any lapse in observing the cardinal rules laid down for nursing cases known, or presumed to be, infectious.

Indeed, it seemed at first ominous when, two weeks later, I complained of increasing langour and a lack of appetite. Soon, however, I became conscious of a heaviness in the pit of my stomach, as if a huge suet dumpling was resisting digestion. Then the colour of my excretions changed, and the whites of my eyes took on a yellowish hue. I looked bilious. I felt bilious.

'Hepatitis and jaundice,' said the doctor, and admitted me to hospital.

'A severe case,' pronounced the specialist. 'No wonder. I understand you've had viral hepatitis before, during the war, a common occurrence in those years. I'm afraid you'll be with us for several weeks.'

I blessed the day when my strength returned and I was able to feed myself again, without having to rest after every spoonful, and to lift myself on to the bedpan without assistance. The day when happiness was mint tea and dry toast, gruel, stewed apples, semolina pudding, and the bouquet of red roses on my locker, which R. never allowed to wilt.

Finally, back at work after an absence of six weeks, my colleagues took a hard look at me.

'What have you done to yourself? You look like a ghost!'

But scarcely had I got used again to commuting and after-work shopping and cooking, than I found myself back in hospital for an operation. And something must have gone wrong in theatre, for on regaining consciousness, and thereafter every waking hour not dulled by injections of morphine, I screamed in pain, at the torture of a tube pulling and tearing mucuous membrane in one of the tenderest parts of my body. In a drugged haze I would look at my mother's shape at my bedside, my faculties clouded, my body possessed by a warm, happy glow, not daring to move, lest the pain should return or the effect of the drug wear off. In lighter moments, my eyes would stray to the pretty cloud of red roses R. had left on my bedside locker.

On the fourth day they operated again, and I stopped screaming.

The first snow was falling, children were opening the twenty-fourth door of their Advent calendars, when I woke after a restless night. My skin was itching madly, and I rose as from a bed of nettles. In the mirror, through puffed-up eyelids, I stared at the bloated landscape of my face and at the blotches covering my trunk.

The doctor diagnosed nettle rash, prescribed antihistamine and soothing applications, and on leaving only just stopped himself from wishing me a 'Happy Christmas'. My mother visited me, loaded with presents and twigs of pine. She shook up my pillows, cooked a meal in my landlady's kitchen and powdered my body. As darkness fell, she lit some candles and tuned the radio to 'Silent Night, Holy Night'.

As rapidly as the rash had broken out, it disappeared again. This is the lot, I thought. I've had my share of doctors and hospitals. Now roll on the good time once more. For surely, by now the stars had moved into a more benevolent constellation. Enthusiastically, I made plans for a spring holiday: a train journey, a Channel crossing, then the Thames valley, Oxford . . .

Braiding golden thoughts I reported back on duty.

Churches were ringing in the New Year when – as in some quintuplication of events – I once again woke to symptoms alien to a young and healthy body: a vicious headache was turning my head into a balloon being pumped full of hot air. My limbs moved sluggishly and my eyes resented the light filtering through the chinks in the curtain.

I went to the bathroom like a sleepwalker. A couple of aspirins, a cold face wash. Gingerly, I shuffled back to bed. An hour later my temperature had risen and my neck felt as stiff as a rod. I telephoned the surgery.

'The doctor will visit you as soon as possible. He's dealing with an emergency right now.'

Another hour passed. My mind was swimming in an opaque sea, my body was on fire, my head resisted every tentative movement. Remembering a lecture at King Edward's, I tried to raise an outstretched leg. I couldn't. Not even a foot high. Not without pain, not without bending it: Kernig's sign, the dreaded test was positive, and I knew what this meant.

I called my landlady.

'I think I'm quite ill, Frau Walter,' I articulated slowly, concentrating on each syllable. 'Would you please ring my cousin at the *Waldkrankenhaus* Spandau. He works as an *Oberarzt*[1] on the Medical Ward. Tell him that I'm running a high temperature, that my neck is stiff and Kernig's sign positive. I also suffer from photophobia and a hell of a headache. And please, call my mother.'

Then everything grew blurred around me. I faintly registered voices and movements in the room, strong arms lifting me on to a stretcher, a shock wave running through my head when one of its poles banged against the staircase wall.

In the street, a wintry breeze fanned my face and cleared my vision.

'Gently, Wilhelm,' said the ambulance man to his mate, as they sat the stretcher down to open the door of the conveyance. I looked into my mother's terrified face, at the bare crowns of chestnut trees outlined against a hard, white sky. Nearby, the tyres of a car screeched, the door of the ambulance banged shut, the siren shrilled, demanding right of way – sounds that made my head feel like a register for decibels. My mother took my hand. '*Mein armes Kind!*' Then my senses misted over again, and I surrendered to the forces which lie beyond the realms of will power and reasoning. Fragments of thoughts remained: 'I

---

1 Senior doctor

don't want to die – please God, not yet!' So did splintered images which had been the darlings of my memory: a garden bursting with colour, with birdsong, with fragrance. Mountain pines reaching for the sky like plumed pallisades, feet stalking over venerable roots and a carpet of moss, pine needles and dappled sunlight. A dinghy on a serene summer lake, passing through a heat haze, my naked body swimming towards a primeval sunset. Winter scenes: Snow falling, snow crunching under my feet, snow trapping sunshine. But now, what a strange sensation? Snow, compacting on my forehead, turning into a sheet of ice, into a compress that cools the furnace behind it . . .

A voice,

'She's come round.'

'Am I going to die?' I asked my cousin, when professional hands had performed a lumbar puncture and made me comfortable in a darkened room, in a bed from which the pillows had been removed.

I sensed fractional hesitation in my cousin's reply.

'Not if I can help it,' he said with tonic cheerfulness. And, reassuring the frightened patient, 'Now, Marianne, no more morbid thoughts! Right now you may be very ill, but I'm sure you'll be out of hospital before the first daffodils are out.'

'But spring is still months away!' I moaned.

My white-coated relative took my hand.

'You've caught a nasty virus, Marianne. But just as Rome wasn't built in one day, so the disease needs time to burn itself out.'

'What exactly is wrong with me? Mind you, I have a good idea. Not long ago I nursed a patient . . . '

My cousin's smile would have encouraged a non-swimmer to dive into the deep end of a pool.

'You've got meningitis. The lab report has just confirmed it. There are also symptoms of encephalitis, quite common with your condition. Also, my neurological examination shows a sensory deficit in your right leg, which tempts one, in a differential diagnosis, to think of a muscular involvement normally encountered in poliomyelitis. But you are strong. We'll get you through. And now, *liebes Kusinchen*, I want you to stop worrying. Rest, sleep . . . '

As the door shut, and the cathedral light of the room enveloped me, I drifted back into feverland.

Busy feet and cheerful voices sounded an early reveille. Sips of tea, a wash, a change of nightdress – ministrations which returned pleasant sensations to hot or flaccid muscles and a degree of alertness to the mind. The curtains were opened just wide enough to drive the blackness from the room.

Some time later, perhaps hours or days – time moves capriciously in the hinterland of feverish wanderings – the ward sister entered my room with a bouquet of twelve red roses.

'Some admirer you've got, Fräulein Gaertner! The English gentleman sends his love. I'm afraid I had to tell him that you will not be allowed any visitors for some time.'

As the weeks went by, the result of further lumbar punctures confirmed a steady improvement in the appearance of my cerebro-spinal fluid and my general condition. I swallowed tons of vitamin tablets, pillows were gradually restored, curtains opened wider. On my bedside table, the scent of roses tempted nurses to put their noses to long-stemmed blooms. My mother was allowed to visit me, so was R., who would regularly turn up at visiting hours.

During my first assisted walking effort I found myself dragging my right leg, in which bones and muscles seemed to have turned to jelly.

'A weakness of the calf muscle,' said the Professor. 'It will improve with exercise.'

That night, when the corridor was quiet, I got out of bed, willing my leg into coordination. But it would not obey. I cried, I shouted at it from within my anger:

'You will, leg! You will, one day!'

I was sitting up in bed, listening to my small radio, when a letter from David and Irene arrived. They had bought a Mallorcan villa not far from Palma, which they were in the process of furbishing with a view to taking in English and German guests for bed and breakfast or half-board.

'We'll be opening in mid-March,' wrote David, 'taking up to eight guests. The first bookings have arrived. We're quite excited. You should see the view from the terrace down to the sea. It is stupendous! We also have a Spanish maid who cooks excellent Paella, a Spanish dog without a pedigree and a well in the back-yard. If you have nothing better to do, Marianne, why not join us down here for the season? You could, if you like, prepare and serve breakfast, help with the shopping and, if you have any energy left, keep an eye on my book-keeping. I'd give you some pocket-money and pay for your return fare. Write and tell us that you will come . . . '

'Arriving in time for opening,' I wrote back, and asked my mother to buy me a copy of *A Spanish Basic Course*. Then I per-suaded my right leg to accompany me on a walk down the corridor.

It was mid-February.

By the time I was discharged from hospital, I had acquired a working knowledge of Spanish.

'Incredible!' cried the nurses, but the professor knew better.

'Your brain, my dear, those little grey cells, they've had a long enforced rest. As a result, they're now absorbing new stimuli like blotting paper.'

He then prescribed sunshine, to put colour into my cheeks, and exercise to activate the lazy muscles of my affected leg.

On the eve of my departure from Berlin, R. treated me to dinner at the Officers' Club, where a three-man band played nostalgic dance tunes.

'I shall miss you,' he stated, as if he were asking the waiter for the bill. But then he was a man who was unable to express his feel-ings in words. I suddenly realized that I might never see my so utterly dependable, generous weekend companion and bedside visitor again – the man whose inner self, even in the most intimate and relaxed hours had remained as elusive to me as higher mathematics at school.

On probing into the prospects of a *Wiedersehen*, R. did not mince his words.

'Who knows? In my job you're here today and gone tomorrow. East West relations have worsened lately. Like the rest of my colleagues I have to be prepared to leave at a few hours' notice.'

'Here today and gone tomorrow', an echo returning from a great distance in the past.

IO

Mallorca, Island of Calm

'If you want to escape from the world's hustlings,
to realize that there exists on earth eternal spring-time
and flowering trees; if you want to get nearer to
the stars, go to the island of calm.'
Rusiñol (Island of Calm, 1908)

Mallorca, 1955

A chilly April wind was making Berliners turn up their coat
collars, when a propeller plane carried me into a fully-blown
Mallorcan spring, and into temperatures more befitting an
English or German summer.

A sun-tanned David and Irene, a porter at their heels, were
waiting for me at Palma Airport.

'Welcome to Mallorca!'

The sun stood in a cloudless sky, the air was soft, and in the
distance a strip of silver revealed the proximity of the Mediterranean. I felt a new chapter of my life opening up.

David's old Riley took us past windmills and blossoming
almond trees, along Palma's busy sea-front promenade and a
narrow, winding coast road to Calamayor, a small cove at the
foot of a ravine. A huge tongue of grassland, dotted with
gnarled trees, pushed inland from the pebbly beach up to the
steeply rising terrain on which perched a few white villas in a
belle-vue scene of fragrance and serenity.

A twisting unmade road led to the Villa Miramar. Built in
Spanish style, with green shutters and a terrace overlooking the
sea, it was surrounded by stunted rose bushes, dwarfed shrubs,
giant cacti and oleander trees. On both sides of the house, steps
rose to a shady concrete backyard in which an ornamental well
with bucket, chain and pump handle, a clothes-line pegged with

washing and a whiff of cooking oil formed a realistic backdrop.

Pepi, the mongrel and self-appointed guardian of the villa, stopped barking and sniffed the stranger in canine acceptance. Outside the kitchen, seated on a low stool, a Spanish maid, who could have stepped out of a crowd scene in *Carmen*, was peeling prawns with southern dexterity.

'This is Musset,' said David.

'Buonas dias!'

'Buonas dias!' Musset replied, smiled and cracked open another pink crustacean.

Inside, guest-rooms and a dining-room were grouped around a large hall in which a high ceiling and a stone-tiled floor created an atmosphere of cool spaciousness. An arched door led on to a terrace and into the blinding midday light which, unless protected by sun-glasses, did not encourage one to cast one's eyes over the bay and the sheet of silver that merged seamlessly with the horizon.

Three functionally-furnished bedrooms, two of which were no larger than a convent cell, formed the basement at front garden level. Windows looked out onto the garden and over the sea.

'This is your room, Marianne,' said David. 'I'm afraid you'll have to pass through our bedroom. I hope you won't find this, eh, awkward. The other single room has been booked.'

Was this the proverbial fly in the ointment? I wondered. A room without direct access, adjoining the most intimate chamber of a young married couple? But then I was delighted with the view, which would afford me frames of southern dawns and sunsets, of the ever-changing mood of the sea and – my heart jumped at the thought of it – starlit skies. And once again the child in me remembered seafarer's tales: of the moon spreading an irridescent carpet over calm waters and, when the tides were right, revealing to a lone deck-watch the spectral emergence of Neptune and his aquatic court . . .

Irene cut through my musings.

'Marianne, you said you were an early riser. Perhaps you wouldn't mind getting things going in the morning and serve breakfast. Musset lives out, and she doesn't come in before ten. David and I are both night-owls. I mean, we would both still be asleep when you get up . . . perhaps at seven?'

'And we were wondering,' ventured David, 'whether as a

trained nurse you could give Irene her daily injection, so that we needn't run down to the clinic for it. I'm sure the doctor would have no objections. You see, she isn't quite over the hill yet. Her right lung . . . '

'No trouble at all,' I said, and I reassured them that after four years of nursing I had perfected the art of giving injections, even with a blunt needle.

'I'll teach you some Spanish,' said David, when Irene was out of earshot. 'It'd be a great help if you could go down to the local market once or twice a week for fish and fresh fruit. Once the guests start arriving, Irene and I shall have little time to breathe.'

Proud of having acquired a fair vocabulary in my self-taught Spanish crash course, including figures up to one thousand, I confronted David as if he were a market stall-holder and I a Mallorcan housewife.

'*Quero dos libras de manzanas e cinco naranjas. Cuanto es? Trescientas cincuenta pesetas? Aqui, quinientas. Ah, perdone, creo que el cambio no está bien!*' I took a deep breath. 'How am I doing?'

'Bravo!' cried David and heartily applauded my act. 'I had no idea that you could speak Spanish. What an asset you're gong to be in our household – and to our budget!' And later, over a lunch of *sopa mallorquina* and deep fried *gambas*, 'We're expecting our first guests at the weekend.'

I woke at dawn. I jumped out of bed, threw open the shutters and looked spellbound at the lovely spectacle of the rising sun throwing a pink hue over the calm sea. But there was no time to wait for the whitening light to encrust it with silver, no time to listen to bird song. I grabbed my swimsuit, stole through my friends' bedroom, risking a glance at the couple locked in sleep, and limped down to the beach. The water, though still on the chilly side, was clear, its mock waves breaking softly on the deserted beach. As I swam daringly towards the open sea, my eyes squinting at the emboldening sun, and conscious of being, at this hour, a tiny human speck in the wide expanse of water, I experienced another of those moments which I knew would

---

1 'I should like two pounds of apples and five oranges. How much is it? Three hundred fifty pesetas? Here are five hundred. Excuse me, but I think you didn't give me enough change!'

keep forever in a special repository of my memory.
experienced another of those moments which I knew would
  Back at the house, with instructions still fresh in my mind, I
made a fire in the range and boiled water for coffee and eggs. I
scooped icy-cold butter into a saucer, heated rolls until crisp,
dished out jam and marmalade and set three places on the terrace.
Soon the smell of fresh coffee lured David and Irene upstairs.

  'Bless you, Marianne!' said Irene, still in her dressing-gown
and looking like a Meissen figurine. 'Breakfast served on the
terrace. What a treat! We'd better make the best of it while we
can. Next week this will be the guests' prerogative.'

  'As from today, we are in business,' announced David a few
days later. Our first guests are the English travel writer S P B
Mais and his wife and daughter. I suppose I'd had better make it
clear to the ladies that women in shorts and slacks are still
frowned upon in the streets, and that Spanish law makes it an
offence to wear a bikini on the beach. Not that Spanish males
would mind,' he added, stroking his timid moustache and
smiling one of his roguish smiles.

  I had never read anything by the allegedly well-known writer,
and David explained that he was a prolific holiday scribe with
several published titles to his credit.

  Soon after the family's arrival, Mr Mais, a shortish, greying
man, established himself with wiry energy in the small basement
room. He pushed the table under the window, placed paper,
pens and books into a waiting position and expressed his hope
that he would not wake us when rising in the morning, which –
as was his habit when working on a book – might be as early as
three o'clock or whenever he might wish to seek the morning
air, in order to dispel writers' block. This said, he set out to find
a Bar in Calamayor which flung its door open to workmen and
early risers for coffee and Campari. His wife, Imogen, and
daughter Lalage, made themselves comfortable in the grandest
Spanish-style room of the villa, and for the next three weeks
would leave their lord and master to his creative pursuits, unless
invited to accompany him to the island's beauty spots or to
Palma's Borné.

  An initial tour of the Borné's attractions under David's

guidance and subsequent lone explorations of life on both sides of the tree-lined paseo, where the locals still outnumbered tourists, had inspired Mais to remain cloistered and write for a whole day. The experience, he said, had indeed provided him with material for several pages of his book.

'A splendid promenade,' he summed up his impressions over dinner. 'You can meditate or doze under those magnificent bower trees, and from under the awning of a bar, sipping coffee or camapri, you can watch life passing by.' He grinned, '. . . especially the pretty señoritas.'

'Hear, hear!' cried David, which prompted Irene, playfully to poke her husband's ribs with a dessert spoon.

'A splendid promenade,' Mais repeated. 'In the bars tapas are free and drinks cold. At the El Tuñel they make the best tortillas, at Rudi's Pedro's guitar and the regulars' sing-song will lift any surly spirit. And where, I ask you, can you meet more interesting British expatriates than at the Formentor Bar?' He looked around to make sure of an attentive audience. 'You know, in his Island of Calm, Rusiñol called the Borné the yolk of Palma, its meridian, its heart and soul.'

David muttered his own appreciation of the Borné, but Mais was already devoting himself single-mindedly to Irene's excellent flan – the Spanish version of a *crème caramel*.

Later, over coffee and liqueurs, David's turn came.

'According to my sources, Mallorca may well be on the brink of some explosive tourist developments. They say, property prices will soar in the coming years, and so will land prices. At the moment you can still rent a modest villa for £12–15 a month, but it might not be long before you pay the same amount for one square yard of building land. And who knows, in a few years, today's prices may look like giveaways.'

Mais started scribbling into his notebook, which I suspected he did not part with even in bed or in the bathroom. David however, encouraged by his guest's fact-gathering, rambled on about builders and land speculators who were finding the prospect of a tourist boom on Mallorca singularly attractive. A prospect, he said, which had many local businessmen rubbing their hands, but which absolutely appalled the true afficionados of the island.

Mais closed his notebook to air his disgust.

'The very idea is repellent. Fancy, Mallorca being swamped by tourists. Bars, beaches and the *Borné* resembling Blackpool on a hot August weekend. God have mercy! Rusiñol would turn in his grave. It would mean a rape of his island of calm, a rape, too of that "eastern solemnity and silence", of which George Sand spoke in her memoirs.'

'I hate to think what a tourist run on Mallorca would do to Valldemosa,' said the latest arrival, Fräulein Peters, a spinster-ish piano teacher from Stuttgart, who professed to have been lured to the island not so much by the sun or the agreeable prospect of a week's utter repose, but – as a devotee of Chopin's music – by an inner urge to visit the Carthusian monastery where the consumptive composer and pianist had spent one winter at the side of George Sand, his friend, nurse and lover.

'Imagine, hordes of people trampling around their cells and touching his piano with sweaty hands, just to tell their folks at home how close they had come to the maestro's instrument – people who might never even have heard a single bar of his music!'

Fräulein Peters closed her eyes in distress, and it was clear to me that she would lose no time in erecting her own shrine to Frederic Chopin.

'Here's something for your notebook, Mr Mais,' suggested David. 'Apparently, the local Guardia fear that with a rising influx of foreigners Palma's prison might no longer stand empty. Crime so far is virtually unknown on the island.'

'Ah,' said Mais, stretching the vowel like an elastic band, 'I'm afraid my book won't help. You see, I'm writing a glowing eulogy on the island's charm.'

Laughter, drinks on the house. Outside, the stars had come out, and the fireflies were dancing between the backcloth of the night and the light of the full moon. No sound tore at the fabric of the hour, except for the distant murmur of the sea and the chatter of the cicadas. The mild, fragrant air embraced me like a lover, and I felt a little jealous of the conjugal happiness which David and Irene were free to give each other on nights like these.

'By the way, David,' said Mais next morning, 'I phoned Robert

Graves, and he asked me to come over. I hear he's working hard on a translation of *Lucan*, but one of his daughters is taking part in Saturday's Ballet at Palma's *Teatro*, and he'll be attending the performance. Why don't we all go along? Classical ballet, Graves said. Not that this is my favourite art form. But the evening is supposed to be something of a family affair. It might be interesting, and I could arrange for him to meet you afterwards.'

'Excuse me, but who is Robert Graves?' I asked Mais who, armed with camera, straw hat and notebook, was waiting for his ladies to accompany him on another excursion that might hopefully yield material for the next chapter of his book.

'My dear girl . . . ' he began, as if the achievements of the said man of letters equalled those of Shakespeare, or the questioner was a complete ignoramus. 'Ah, but then you're German,' he checked himself and, as for an obituary, listed the works of Robert Graves and his impact on English literature.

There was, I thought, no end to what I still had to learn — even on Mallorca. And it was only April.

For me, the evening at the *Teatro* offered no more than mild entertainment. No reknowned ballet company was the attraction, but the pupils of the local ballet school, and instead of a famous prima ballerina, a wisp of a girl in pink voile danced the Sugar Plum Fairy. The audience, consisting mainly of parents, generously applauded every *pas-de-deux* and choreographic group effort. In the interval, the ladies showed off Catalan elegance, beautifully crafted jewellery and matriarchal pride. Among the males, of whom many wore black ties, I noticed fine aquiline features, the vain glances of ageing torero-types, the comfortable girths of siesta-loving señors, Cervantean foreheads and at least one goatee beard. This was Palma's upper crust society, Mallorcans living above the bread-oil-and-olive line. Parental exhibitionism was perhaps as manifestly in evidence as at similar venues in London, Paris and Rome, or at some ritual dancing display of tribal youngsters in outer Mongolia or deepest Africa.

I was introduced to Robert Graves after the performance. Strands of greying hair escaped from under a wide-brimmed felt hat. Sharp, provocative eyes cursorily glanced at me. A hand touched mine like a sea breeze. Wearily, but affably, he acknowledged a greeting here and there, a man sure of his own worth, who could afford to select his friends and did not have to court his public. I thought it strange, however, that he paid little attention to the loquacious Mr Mais, as if he resented the latter's chumminess or – in the loftier world of the *literati par excellence* – he had perhaps no more time to spare for a travel writer.

Mais, oblivious of not being accorded equal footing, chatted on regardless, before Graves tossed a 'Good night' at us and strode away like Claudius, Emperor and God.

Back at the villa that night Mais revealed that he had made contact with the Princess of Holstein, and that she had invited him to her Palma residence. Some travel writers, I mused, certainly knew how to spot the famous and those with a high social profile in a foreign locale. They realized that a little shoulder-rubbing never came amiss, and that human interest paragraphs spiced up what was essentially a straightforward travel-writing formula.

I soon settled into an agreeable routine. On rising, I first listened to the dawn chorus in the garden and, with an inner repose akin to prayer, communed with the sea in its waking light before preparing breakfast for the guests. After my own *desayuno*[1] which I had in the backyard, peasant-fashion, I might go to the Terreno market, taking my pick of fresh fish, fruit and vegetables. I helped around the house, laid the dining-table and, in the evenings, served the dinners which Irene, an accomplished cook, dished out in the steaming kitchen, and for which we joined our guests. In between duties, I sun-bathed on the terrace, swam off the rocks below the Puchet Bar or fetched water from the well, whenever the tap water had ceased running. And it was not long before the muscles of my right leg regained their former tone and my body glowed with a healthy tan; not long before I tried to choke emotional needs aroused in the seductive atmosphere of Mallorcan nights, by ploughing through *La Filosofía de la Felicidad*, a philosophical treatise on

---

1 Breakfast

Happiness and a guaranteed sleep-inducer on hot nights.

By the time the Mais family left, Bill, an Irishman in his forties, had added himself to our threesome.

A quiet, easy-going man, he lived in a penthouse on Palma's Borné, drove an Italian Convertible and confessed to a passion for Rachmaninoff's piano concertos. Although he was rumoured to have made his fortune on the Irish pools, a question mark remained in British expatriate circles over the acquisition of his wealth, no doubt kindled by his pipe-smoking reticence and a refusal to let anyone into his past. While soaking up the island's sun, toying with the idea of buying a villa and a yacht, and studying the investment market, he seemed to feel a strange need for friends under whose roof he could divest himself of whatever shadows had pursued him to the island. Unpredictable in his comings and goings, seldom, if ever, being on time, and sometimes not turning up at all, Bill was an odd creature, obsessed with his personal freedom, yet generous and good company. With his startling blue eyes and understatement of Irish charm, he posed a serious threat to any lone female listening in his company to the erotic overtones of Rachmaninoff's Second Piano Concerto, or yearning for more than the loving touch of a Mallorcan summer breeze.

In between the departure and arrival of guests there was often a welcome breathing space which the four of us, squeezed into Bill's racer, used to explore the island: Deya, the artists' village, where scattered white houses snuggled picturesquely into the hills, overlooking orchards and olive plantations; where Robert Graves lived with his family during Palma's torrid heat, and painters and scribes could be seen flocking to their favourite bars in white floppy jackets and adventurous hats. At Inka, we watched a bullfight, and ate suckling pig from the spit; we sauntered through white-washed villages which, save for a scrawny dog, or a goat standing in the shade of a tree in a stupor, looked deserted during the siesta hours. One day, we visited Valldemosa.

The midday sun was beating down when we arrived at the Carthusian Monastery which commanded a grand view over gardens, obelisk-shaped cypresses and bluish olive trees to the misted-over coastline. But there was relief from the heat behind the massive walls, and Chopin and George Sand's former quarters were cool and airy.

Sparsely furnished, with niches for candles, and a white rose adorning the composer's piano, the cells led on to a stone-partitioned terrace on which, partly shaded by a verdant pergola, standard rose trees, dwarf cypresses, potted plants and generations of needle or dome-shaped cacti formed a miniature garden of magical quality likely to enthral the least romantic of visitors.

A flag-stoned path encouraged a walk-about. For precious moments I found myself alone, conscious of the rare blend of beauty, tranquillity and summer perfume acting like an opiate on my soul. In the stillness, which the humming of insects and the solitary cry of a bird magnified, rather than violated, I listened, mesmerized, to the ghostly keyboard sounds of an Etude issuing from Chopin's piano, feeling myself delightfully imprisoned by some trick of the senses, until the footsteps of my companions returned me to reality.

And how could I ever forget our outing to La Calobra – the terrifying drive down a narrow, winding road and through a rocky wilderness which, here and there, was softened by a golden fleece of broom or by a lusty torrent spouting over sheer rock among clouds of white spume? Or the emergence of the blue and silver-toned sea at the foot of the petryifying descent? The bar-ristorante shaded by a bamboo awning, the empty tables, the smell of fish and cooking oil . . . ?

'Let's have a drink before we order lunch,' said Bill, and the two men slumped down into wicker chairs.

'Marianne and I would like a swim first,' said Irene, and we scrambled off in search of a sandy cove.

Irene saw it first: a narrow entrance, a mere cleft between overhanging cliffs, a track no wider than a man's shoulders, running through a defile, along which the rocks rose higher and higher. Like children, who had come upon a secret path into fairyland, we penetrated deeper into the majestic world of once sea-buffeted, sea-shaped diluvian rocks. Suddenly, light, echoes, a transparent sea-water pool shot through with sun-beams, a bed of smooth, disk-shaped pebbles, visible as through a magnifying glass.

'How absolutely idyllic!' cried Irene.

Having aired my own enchantment, I took off my clothes.

Gingerly, I stepped into the water, in which to wear a swimsuit would have been a sacrilege.

'This is paradise,' I said, and with gentle swimming strokes allowed the sun-heated water to caress my body.

Irene followed suit. And the magic of the place was such that we bathed in silence, picking up pebbles and running them through our fingers like pearls, or floating on our backs, eyes closed, our nipples buoying up, only to be washed over by the water again and again. Or diving, eyes open, through a world of liquid glass, like fish, like water nymphs . . .

There were some wonderful beaches on the island, often reached by a narrow path or by tracking through scrubland and pine copses. Here the sand was virginal, the sea crystal-blue or lime-coloured, and the sole occupancy of such coastal stretch shared only with Pepi, the mongrel, a priceless privilege.

There were times when I wished the life I was leading would just run on and on, babbling like a brook, unchecked, a never-ending, slow-paced season of sun, sand and sea, fragrant nights and cool drinks on terraces. I felt good. I felt young. I was happy in a solitary way. But I was no longer a child. I had learnt about the fickleness and instability of happiness and of all good things. Besides, although I was still cutting my way through the philosophical jungle of *La Filosofia*, I realized that one day the record of Rachmaninoff's Second would sound scratched and my sun-lazed mind and body would demand a greater challenge. I might even long for a rain shower and verdant pastures, for the coolness of an English cathedral or the cosiness of a warm room behind iced-up windows.

That night I critically looked at my naked sun-tanned body in the mirror. I stroked my firm, hungry breasts. I put a hand on my flat belly. Would it ever bulge with the weight of expectant motherhood? Would I ever come truly 'home'? Suddenly I saw time racing past and myself, trapped in mortality, making a desperate bid to slow it down. I sat at my window, staring at the illuminated sky. What was my role on this earth, and would I ever know the completion of my self?

David and Irene's bedtime voices drifted through the door. Then it grew quiet, but for the creaking of bed springs.

I had just turned thirty.

S P B Mais, chronicler of local scenery and people, had collected some astonishing facts about Don Juan March, the 'Nuffield' of Mallorca and reputedly the richest and most influential man on the island. The señor, a fine figure of a man, who owned the island of Dragonera, a vineyard and a fabulous villa built against the rocks of Pollensa Bay, was not only a farmer, an art collector, a Doctor of Chemistry and a close friend of Carmen, the only daughter of El Generalissimo Franco, but a shrewd businessman whose affairs required him to keep in constant touch with Paris, Rome and Madrid. Rumour would have it that he was the father of twenty-one children.

I was introduced to Don Juan at the Formentor Bar in Palma, where he was conducting the day's affairs from a wicker chair, sipping an *apérativo* and portraying the self-confidence of the wealthy, the alertness of a stock-market operator and the power of a feudal lord. He was accompanied by his secretary, a sinewy man of harassed and dyspeptic looks, who sat in his chair as on a red hot girdle. Within minutes, a telephone call and a few snappy instructions from his master sent him racing off in a shiny Cadillac to wherever business lay.

'The three of you must come and have dinner with me some time,' said Don Juan, picking up his newspaper, thus intimating that he was ready to resume the study of the day's stock market. A very private smile touched me as we duly rose, before Don Juan affected a bow to the ladies and addressed David, business-like.

'I'll have my secretary get in touch with you. *Adiós!*'

The invitation came a month later, when Mallorca was broiling in the sun. Fortunately at this time of the year, which only saw a scattering of intrepid travellers to the island, no guests had booked into the Villa Miramar, and the three of us were free to accept not only an invitation to dinner, but also for an overnight stay at our host's villa.

'Don Juan is anxious that you shouldn't have to drive home along those hair-pin bends at night,' said the secretary, who had personally called at the 'Miramar'. 'Would you please meet Don Juan in the bar of the Formentor Hotel.' This said, he rushed off again as if the hounds of Hell were at his heels.

'A perfect candidate for a stroke or stomach ulcers,' said David, and sat down in the shade with the newspaper, *Corriere*, a long drink by his side.

The Formentor Hotel ranked as Mallorca's top 'inn' for rich and discerning holiday-makers. A beautiful sandy beach, edged by conifers, lay deserted in the fading light of the evening. From the hotel's patio, a tiered garden extended down to the sea, and judging by the impact on the visitors's olfactory nerves, a host of flowers and blooming shrubs were releasing their fragrance into the sultry air.

Don Juan arrived well after nine o'clock. He greeted us like long-lost friends, ordered drinks, discussed with David the strength of the English pound and the adverse effect a tourist boom would have on indigenous culture and land prices. He handed a plate of fried octopus and calamares around and, as a man of the world, did not forget to engage the ladies in conversation.

I was beginning to feel as if I had not eaten for days, when our host rose and, stepping out on to the terrace, invited me to follow him. David went to order a guest round of *Manzanillas* and Irene removed herself to the ladies' powder-room.

'Mariana,' began Don Juan, putting a bold arm around my shoulders, 'how would you like to come and live up at my villa? . . . To look after my younger children,' he added hastily when I looked at him sharply. 'You'd have every comfort . . . a fine salary, good food, a lovely room . . . '

I was lost for words. I felt honoured. I felt tempted. But I also sensed the presence of a man not used to lengthy courting, whether of women or prospective business partners. Like an accountant I wondered how the intangibles involved in such an offer might affect the balance sheet of my future.

The increasing pressure on my shoulders decided the issue. I thought of the army of children the charming señor had allegedly sired, and I spoke of my loyalty to Irene and David.

'I understand,' said Don Juan, 'but any time you should wish to change your mind . . . '

It had turned eleven, when we sat down for dinner in an airy palatial room, surrounded by paintings of the Spanish school and by servants who seemed to walk on felt soles. The *gazpacho*, the seafood platter, and the final poem of a mango and orange dessert were true to a millionaire's table and a Catalan palate.

Coffee and liqueurs were served as we sank into soft-cushioned wicker settees on the patio. Here, night stole around us, and honeyed scents from the garden were robbing wakefulness. Slowly, conversation began to falter, drowsiness to creep upon the non-Spanish guests.

'Tomorrow I'll show you the new villa I'm having built,' said Don Juan, as David and Irene asked permission to retire. I was about to follow suit, when a firm hand held me fixed to my seat.

'Don't go yet, Mariana!'

A deep, mellifluous voice, trying to disguise the impression that it was used to having orders obeyed without the flicker of an eyelid, and personal wishes, however eccentric or uncere-monious, granted with a smile.

In my mind's eye I saw twenty-one children lined up for a roll-call. And where in this stately residencia was the mistress of the house?

'Forgive me, Don Juan,' I said, 'but I'm very tired.'

With all the grace I could muster, I blamed the heat, the lateness of the hour, the Spanish wine.

'*Muchas gracias, señor, por una sera perfecta.*'[1]

Don Juan's smile was equally gracious, and he kissed my hand as if I had been a *principessa* or – come to think of it – the mother of one of his sons.

However, not leaving anything to chance, I turned the key on my bedroom door that night.

The private corniche road had been hewn out of sheer rock and cut through dense pine growth. It ended high up on the cliffs of an idyllic bay. Rocks soaring straight from the sea ensured total privacy, while access to the villa was through an imposing wrought-iron gate guarded by two teeth-baring Afghan hounds.

The view from the house, which from any ordinary window would have been breathtaking, gained in dramatic effect from the total glazing of its sea-front facade. For here, glass panels spanning the entire width of each room, afforded spectacular wide-screen vistas miles from the public eye. Given to an adventurous imagination I wondered whether the subscriber to this architectural feat would find it an erotic experience to

---

1 'Thank you for a perfect evening'

wander about stark naked in his bedroom, curtains wide open, or to make love before the voyeurish eyes of the sea, and the sun or moon. Whether, by dint of an optical illusion, such constructional triumph would allow the owner of this de luxe domicile to lie in his transparent bath as in the blue waters of the Mediterranean below, or watch the sea in its changing moods from his seignorial toilet seat. And who knows what inspirations, what fantasies might befall a man who looked at the outside world from behind a glass façade.

Don Juan put an end to my observations and bold speculations.

'Do you like the house, Mariana? Well, any time you should wish to change your mind . . . '

David and Irene had gone to bed, and I was on the brink of sleep when the telephone rang. Irene knocked at my door.

'Marianne, Don Juan March has invited us to dinner over at Tito's. He says there's a big party going. Some famous names among the guests. Perhaps we'd like to meet them. He would wangle us inside. D'you want to come?'

'When?'

'Now.'

'What, tonight?'

'Well, you know how spontaneous their invitations are. Anyway, they never sit down for dinner before ten or eleven.'

What time is it?'

'Ten o'clock.'

I yawned.

David's voice,

'Come on the two of you. Let's make an effort. March is a useful man to know on the island. We can't just brush off an invitation however impulsive or late at night.'

I took the curlers out of my hair, splashed cold water on my face and donned a sleeveless cotton dress held up by narrow shoulder straps. It was a balmy night, bereft of any sea breezes, and the thought of a Spanish midnight dinner, when one's mind and body were already pitched to sleep, positively lacked appeal.

Tito's looked out over a dark sea which reflected a myriad of lights. Through the open windows there came the sound of voices, the clatter of dishes and the first bars of Mallorcan music. A man approached us.

'Are you Juan's guests?' he asked in an Oxbridge accent. An old-fashioned lantern shed light on our challenger: a dark club-style blazer, a white open-neck shirt, a red cravat. A deeply-tanned face, a languid smile. Eyes that no longer expected surprises, bluish, mildly searching. A man exuding sensuality as some animal its mating scent. I held my breath. Before me stood the spitting image of Errol Flynn, the famous good-time extrovert, the screen's swashbuckler, adventurer and seducer, the heart-throb of millions of teenagers, shop girls and housewives.

'Hello,' he said, shaking David's hand and kissing Irene's and mine.

For me, the scene was unreal, as if the gentleman and philanderer Flynn had just stepped out from the screen.

Two hefty doorkeepers admitted us to the restaurant and night-club, which was empty except for a party occupying a banquet-length table. A lady of eminently Spanish looks and grande-dame bearing commanded everyone's attention. Don Juan rose to greet us.

'*Holà, amiges*! I see you met Errol outside. I asked him to look out for you and get you past the two bulldogs at the door. He said he needed to stretch his legs. He's only just come ashore His yacht is anchored off Terreno.'

'I thought it might be him,' said David, as casually as if he were used to meeting the screen's Great after brushing his teeth for the night. 'Is he filming locally?'

'No, just cruising in between films, restless wanderer that he is.'

'It was kind of you . . . ' began David, but the millionnaire was already heading towards a table at a respectable distance from the central stage, but which still afforded a clear view of the diners.

'I hope you don't mind sitting by your own. It is rather a private affair over there, you know. I told Carmen's security men that you were friends of mine. The place is closed to the public tonight.'

Our eyebrows shot up questioningly.

'Ah, I forgot to tell you, our guest of honour is Franco's daughter, Carmen. We're celebrating her birthday. And now, *amiges*, excuse me while I rejoin the party. Order anything you like for dinner. You're my guests.' A lordly lifting of a hand summoned the waiter.

For two hours the three of us hugged the table in somnolent conversation, our eyes frequently focussing on the table where party gaiety never turned excessive, just as if the Spanish dictator himself was keeping an eye on his daughter's company. We ordered omelettes, which came delightfully fluffy and the size of dinner plates, but feeling our insides slightly out of gear at this hour, contented ourselves with drinking mineral water, which prompted the waiters to pass comments on *'los Ingléses'* who did not know how to have a good time at someone else's expense.

Well after midnight, a Flamenco dancer of sultry yet haughty mien, a red rose between her teeth, took to the stage and performed her act with much clicking of castanets and staccato heel tapping. Carmen applauded royally.

By the time we returned to the 'Miramar', dawn had turned the horizon pink and the air had a lovely crisp quality. I fell asleep instantly, only to wake to the clamour of guests demanding their breakfast. But then my account of the night's outing ironed out angry brows, particularly those of two ladies from Stockholm, who seemed intrigued by the titillating thought of Errol Flynn having stepped ashore so close to Calamayor.

'*Perdone, señorita.*'

I blinked at the young man in bathing trunks and sunglasses, and decided that his looks and polite overture ruled out the possibility of molestation. Not waiting for an answer, he sat down, cross-legged, beside me.

'*Me nombre es Filippo. Como se llama?*'

'Marianne.'

'*Es Inglès?*'

'No, *Alemán.*'

'*Ha! Habla Español?*'

'*Non mucho.*'

'*Ich nicht sprechen Deutsch.*'

'*Parlez-vous français?*'

'*Oui, mais pas beaucoup.*'

'English?'

'*Si.* I had English nanny, and I learn at school.'

'Well then,' I said, 'let's stick to English.'

It was a curious beginning for a fleeting romance that was tailored to a Mallorcan summer.

Half-an-hour and a swim later, we talked like old friends, just as if the combination of sun, sand, water and the island's inescapable holiday spirit invited intimate conversation. And it was not long before I saw Eros gambolling on the beach, grinning, winking, and sharpening his arrows.

For a week Filippo and I met during the day whenever David and Irene could spare me at the villa. We sun-oiled each other's back, swam and frolicked in the water, or sped on Filippo's hired motorcycle around the island, with myself hanging on to the driver as to dear life itself, and often closing my eyes in sheer panic during a hair-pin descent. At Felantix, over a bottle of local white wine, we exchanged our life histories; at Pueblo, at the village well, we kissed. In the evenings, we danced on the patio of Filippo's smart Terreno hotel, ending up in the garden of the 'Miramar' under midnight skies, watching fireflies and looking out for August's shooting stars.

'Perhaps you'll visit me in Madrid later this year,' said my Spanish gentleman one night, and he talked of his student days at Madrid university, and of his friendship with Don Juan Carlos.

'I've known the Prince for a long time. As children we used to spend every holiday together at the Estoril Palace. We're meeting in Portugal next week, and there's a good chance that Carlos will be attending the Military Academy in Madrid next year.'

There was, I thought, no telling whose path one was likely to cross on the island. One might shake hands, come face to face or share a table with *literati*, film stars and millionaires, and one might even be kissed by a young *Madrileño* who had the Pretender to the Spanish throne for a friend.

At the end of his short holiday, Filippo returned to Madrid, but not before repeating his invitation.

'Do come and visit me, Mariana. The best time would be in October, when my parents will be away in the States for the remainder of the year.' Then came the bait. 'We have a large house and heated swimming pool. I might even take you for a spin to the Estoril . . . '

Aha! said my moral sentinel, when the cats are away, the mice will play in Spain, just as they do elsewhere. And in reply to what had sounded like a jolly offer underlaid with dishonourable intentions, I flashed a non-committing smile at my Spanish *caballero*.

Adiós, Filippo!

Patrick, a guest at the 'Miramar', came from London. A young barrister of Byronic looks and a hobby painter, he confessed to having a passion for French literature and for the paradisiacal colours of Mallorca which, he said, were a painter's dream. Every morning he would set out with his easel and painting paraphernalia, looking suitably bohemian in an old Panama hat and in clothes unlikely to be seen at Lincoln or Gray's Inn.

Patrick courted me over after-dinner drinks, before retiring early, 'to catch the best light of the morning'. And justifying his obsession with the island as one of the most beautiful and potently creative for painters, he quoted from George Sand's *Un Hivers à Mallorque* in his own polished translation, 'Mallorca is the Eldorado of painting. There is picturesque beauty everywhere. It is green Helvetia under a Calabrian sky.' But then he added, 'Of course the lady was here in winter, and not in August, by which time the heat of the sun has bleached or browned much of that lovely green.'

'Let's have a party,' said David, when the last guests had departed in October. 'Dancing, *sangría*, the lot. Our first season has ended. We have even made a few pesetas.'

There was indeed much dancing, singing and *sangría* in the big hall and on the terrace that night. I risked a fiery Paso Doble with handsome Pedro Domecq, son of the sherry king, and watched his American girl friend, of startlingly sophisticated looks, perform a Flamenco Fifth Avenue style. I melted in the arms of Bill who, after staying away from the villa for weeks, allegedly in order to avoid emotional involvement with me, had suddenly turned up, uninvited, yet most welcome. Mallorcan dance music blended with a moonlit sky, putting zest into my limbs and a strange lack of inhibition into my blood, just as if my suitcase stood ready packed. When, I wondered, would the respite from the alien years be over? And was I suffering from nostalgia even before I had turned my back on the island?

Towards the end of October it started raining and the wind blew in hard from the sea. Days for picking up *La Filosofia* again, days for wearing a cardigan and watching the choppy sea. Days, also, to send my thoughts ahead to Berlin.

David made it easy for me.

'Marianne, I think the time has come for you to go home. Irene likes to visit her mother in Munich, and I shall be involved in some business.'

I wrote to R.: 'I'm coming back.'

R. telegraphed: 'Taking overdue leave. Meeting you at Barcelona.'

And there he stood, waiting, as the overnight ferry from Palma docked in Barcelona harbour: R., the very antithesis to Mallorca's sweet summer madness, a champion of sober thought and integrity, the man to whom his friends referred as 'the eternal bachelor', and of whom his enemies said that sooner would a woman manage to crack open a Brazil nut with her bare hands than drive him into wedlock.

A smile appeared on R.'s face, like the sun darting through a shift in the clouds.

'Had a good crossing? Here, let me take your suitcase. The car is parked over there.'

He pointed to the grey Vanguard, the colossus which evoked instant memories of rides along the Havel lakes and through the Grunewald, and of R. patiently chauffeuring me through the city.

'I've booked a hotel room for the night,' he said. 'Tomorrow we'll start back along the coast, then up north through France.'

And later, walking down the Rambla, 'By the way, at the Canadian Mission in Berlin they're looking for a German lady with a good knowledge of English. The job might suit you. The chap in charge told me he'll be holding the post open for you until you get back.'

A thousand miles away in Berlin, a new job was waiting for me. But was I going home?

Epilogue

The Homecoming

1956

Once again, the political atmosphere in Berlin was tense. The popular rising in Hungary had been harshly repressed by Russian forces, and Berliners were wondering if their own city might wake up one morning to Russian tanks droning through the streets. The recent Franco-British air raids over Egypt during the Israeli invasion, and the Soviety Union's threat of military intervention had added a new dimension to the widespread sense of insecurity.

And it did not fail to affect R.

'You realize, Marianne, that I might have to leave Berlin within hours. The political situation . . . '

I went to the window and stared out over a rain and windswept street in which, under the bare trees, all the melancholy of a German November had amassed. I thought of the fear of many West-Berliners that they might find themselves abandoned one morning to Russian and East-German troops, Volkspolizei and political commissars, not unlike the people of Tangermünde, whose British-occupied town, falling victim to Allied concessions east of the river Elbe, had been handed over to the Soviets in 1945 overnight, clandestinely, on a plate.

A new alien world, ruled by the hammer and sickle, loud slogans and political bravura, opened up before me, a world in which one was whispering and looking over one's shoulder again, and freedom of speech and movement had been wiped from the public vocabulary.

At the thought of R. suddenly gone, of our agreeable weekend relationship, and my only link with an English-speaking British-orientated community being severed, perhaps overnight, perhaps without leaving him time to compose a farewell note, a foretaste of that all too familiar state of loneliness whipped up within me a maelstrom of feelings. And if this was not enough, such self-indulgence gave way to other projections.

I saw time racing past to the accompaniment of trumpets, blaring, 'You are thirty-one years old!' I saw myself, a self-professed stranger on native soil and among my own people; I saw alienation waiting for me even in the stillness of my rented room, and boredom in an office stuffed with filing cabinets, application forms and card indices. Why, did not Rilke in his poem, *Der Herbsttag* say:

> 'Wer jetzt kein Haus hat, baut sich keines mehr,
> Wer jetzt allein ist, wird es lange bleiben,
> Wird wachen, lesen, lange Briefe schreiben
> Und wird in den Alleen hin und her
> Unruhig wandern, wenn die Blätter treiben . . . '[1]

The harsh lyricism of the lines touched me where my sensibilities were at their rawest. Quietly, I went into the next room and cried.

Ten minutes had passed, when R. entered and, without uttering a single word, took me in his arms – in the sober light of the grizzly day a movingly intimate gesture for a man like him.

R.'s voice sounded cracked.

'Will you marry me?'

I held my breath and listened to the sudden calm inside me.

'Please,' said R.

And now spring exploded around me – an orchestra of vernal sounds, a powerhouse of budding, blooming and bestirring, an exquisite chaos in which love finally declared itself, and in relinquishing the temporariness of our liaison, opened up our future and firmed the ground under our feet.

I smiled an ecstatic, 'Yes'.

---

[1] 'Who has no house now, will build him no more.
Who is alone now, long will so remain,
will wake, read, write long letters,
and will in the avenues to and fro
restlessly wander, when the leaves are blowing.'

(*The Book of Pictures*)
Transl. H D Herter-Norton

Perhaps winged by a potent breath of that same spring, R.'s thoughts raced ahead.

'Shall we have children?'

I nodded emphatically.

'Two, no, three?'

'Yes, yes,' I cried.

'We'll get married in January. Time for you to apply for British citizenship and for me to complete all the formalities. In the meantime, I shall apply for accommodation. We might get a flat or a house with garden. It'll come fully furnished for married personnel. And first thing tomorrow, you'll give in your notice at work. In the afternoon, we'll go to the Kurfürstendamm and I'll buy you an engagement ring.' R. took a deep breath. 'Let's celebrate tonight. What about dinner in the Mess? Wine, a bottle of Champagne? . . . '

But all I could think of was that the alien years had ended. I had come home.

Copies of the paper back version of

THE NAKED YEARS

are still available. In case of difficulty, copies can be ordered from

54 Rosehill
Torrance
Glasgow
G64 4HF